NAT TURNER'S
SLAVE REBELLION

The American Institute for Marxist Studies (AIMS)
is a non-profit educational, research and biblio-
graphical institute. Its purposes are to encourage
Marxist and radical scholarship in the United
States and to help bring Marxist thought into the
forum of reasonable debate to produce a meaning-
ful dialogue among Marxist and non-Marxist
scholars and writers. Its policy is to avoid sectarian
and dogmatic thinking. It engages in no political
activity and takes no stand on political questions.
It grinds no axe for any group, party, sect, organization.

To these ends it invites the support and participation of all scholars and public-spirited individuals.

NAT TURNER'S
SLAVE REBELLION

By Herbert Aptheker

TOGETHER WITH THE FULL TEXT OF
THE SO-CALLED "CONFESSIONS" OF
NAT TURNER MADE IN PRISON
IN 1831

Published for A.I.M.S. by
HUMANITIES PRESS
New York

Library of Congress Catalog Card Number: 66-18376

Printed in the United States of America

CONTENTS

(The complete text of the Original (1831) Edition of Nat Turner's so-called *"Confessions"*)

FOREWORD

THIRTY YEARS AFTER

There is no book dealing with the revolt of slaves in Southampton County, Virginia, in August, 1831, led by Nat Turner, except that written by William S. Drewry and published more than sixty-five years ago. Of that work sufficient is said in the pages that follow; here it need but be commented that for the truth of the Turner event it would have been better if Drewry had never published.

Toward the close of the 19th century, the young Harvard student William Edward Burghardt Du Bois, was fascinated by the Turner event; encouraged by Professor Albert Bushnell Hart he spent much time studying it. His doctoral thesis, however, was on the suppression of the African slave trade, and Du Bois did not publish any study of Turner. He almost did, though, and therein lies a story.

In the first decade of the twentieth century, the Philadelphia publishing firm of George Jacobs & Co., launched the American Crisis Biography series, under the editorship of the historian, Ellis P. Oberholtzer; the idea of the series, explaining its title, was to produce biographical studies of personalities identified with particularly critical episodes or periods in American history. Du Bois' reputation as a scholar already was well established—in 1896 his Harvard Historical Studies Number I, and in 1899 his study of *The Philadelphia Negro*—University of Pennsylvania Studies Number 14—and in 1903 his masterpiece, *The Souls of Black Folk* had appeared.

Hence, Mr. Oberholtzer asked Dr. Du Bois if he would undertake for the Jacobs series a biography of Frederick Douglass who had died in 1895. Du Bois agreed, and a contract was signed. Word of this agreement, however, got out of the Jacobs office and reached the ears of Booker T. Washington at Tuskegee. Mr. Washington let it be known that he was not pleased with the choice of a biographer for the late Douglass and that a more worthy choice would be—Mr. Washington. This settled that question, and poor Mr. Oberholtzer wrote in evident embarrassment to Dr. Du Bois of the necessary switch in authors for the Douglass book; at the same time, he asked Du Bois to suggest his own choices for biographical treatment.

Dr. Du Bois, put out, but exercising his considerable powers of restraint, reminded the Jacobs firm of their contract, yielded to its decision on Douglass and then stated he wished to produce a volume on either of two subjects: Nat Turner or John Brown!

The Jacobs firm, faced with the problem of Du Bois as an author—he had already launched the terribly radical Niagara Movement—now had to choose between a black insurrectionist or a white one. It chose, of course, the white man; thus did Du Bois' *John Brown* appear (first in 1909) while Du Bois' work on Turner never did get done.

In the heady New Deal days of the '30's, Professor Rayford W. Logan conceived of a Committee whose purpose it would be to erect a monument to the memory of Nat Turner; Dr. Du Bois told the young Logan that he doubted this could be accomplished, but wished him well. Du Bois was right.

At the same time—and also a child of the times—the present writer, who already had seen a good deal of the South and whose main interests for several years had been devoted to U.S. history and especially to the subject of slavery, began a study of what was then conceived generally to be an altogether unique event—a slave insurrection in the United States.

The book now in the reader's hand was written, then, thirty years ago, and accepted as a thesis for the master's degree at Columbia University in February, 1937. Professor Allan Nevins—though perhaps bothered by an overly intense student—was encouraging; particularly helpful at that time was the late Professor William L. Westermann, whose renown rested upon his mastery of ancient slavery but who was fascinated by comparative studies and who especially helped this beginner. For three decades this study has reposed on the shelves of the Columbia library—not unread, I am happy to say—and now, at last, a publisher has decided to give it life.

The bibliography appended hereto is full enough up to the date of its compilation. Additional references to the Turner event itself, to slavery and to the whole history of slave unrest are in the bibliography printed in the present writer's *American Negro Slave Revolts* (first published, 1943) and in the prefatory note to the 1963 edition of that book. In addition, note should be taken of John Lofton's *Insurrection in South Carolina: The Turbulent World of Denmark Vesey* (Yellow Springs, Ohio, 1964, Antioch Press) and the review of that book by the present writer, wherein other sources also are cited (in *Science & Society*, Summer, 1965, XXIX, 374-76). Also meriting attention is the article by Marion D. deB. Kilson, "Towards Freedom: An Analysis of Slave Revolts in the United States," *Phylon*, Summer, 1964, XXV, 175-87.

There have been a few novels, in American literature, which have centered around Negro slave unrest and uprisings. These include Harriet Beecher Stowe's massive two-volume *Dred*, published in 1856. Two years later appeared *The Old Dominion*, from the pen of the English novelist, G. P. R. James, then a consular agent in Richmond. Nothing further of this character appeared until 1899 when Mary Johnston's *Prisoners of Hope* and Pauline C. Bouve's *The Shadows Before* were published.

Then ensued a long interval terminated in 1936 by Arna Bontemps' splendid *Black Thunder*, while in 1944 another excellent work, *The Red Cock Crows*, appeared from the pen of Frances Gaither. Two or three years ago it became known that William Styron was working on a novel in which the Turner uprising would play a major role, but as of this date the book has not appeared. Occasional plays also have had as their themes slave rebellions.

Very recently, almost the entire text of the so-called *Confessions* of Nat Turner was reprinted in the volume edited by Professor Harvey Wish, *Slavery in the South: First-Hand Accounts of the Ante-Bellum American Southland* (N.Y., 1964, Farrar, Straus & Co., pp. 5-22). Unfortunately, in this version the appendices were omitted, thus removing from the eyes of the reader the immediate cost of the effort to the Negro people in the numbers arrested, banished, jailed and executed. Unfortunately, too, in his brief introductory note, Prof. Wish repeats two well-worn errors: one leading the reader to believe that "stringent codes for policing" came *after* the revolt when, in fact, as the work that follows shows, many of them *preceded* the event. Further, Prof. Wish states that the Revolt induced a "faltering" in "the flourishing emancipation movement in the South." It is highly dubious that there *ever* was in the South what may be accurately described as a "flourishing emancipation movement;" certainly none such existed by the time Turner rebelled.*

Reflecting the obvious contemporary relevance of all evidences of Negro militancy and mass action in the past is the fact that in a recent number (July, 1965) *The Negro Digest* reprinted in full an edition of the Nat Turner *Confessions* issued in Petersburg, Virginia in 1881.

Thirty years after its original composition, then, and one hundred and thirty-five years after the event, appears this detailed examination of the slave rebellion led by Nat Turner.

December, 1965

---

*This ancient myth that the South, or that Virginia, was on the verge of emancipation and would have acted in this direction but for the Turner rebellion dies hard. Its refutation is in the work that follows. It is repeated not only by Professor Wish, as above, but also even more recently by Prof. Louis Filler in his edition of *Wendell Phillips on Civil Liberties and Freedom* (N.Y., 1965, Hill & Wang), p. 108 n.

INTRODUCTION

The 1830's were a revolutionary period throughout the world. People everywhere were agitating, striving, dying for a greater share in determining governmental policies or for national liberation. Quite naturally, the press of the United States was favorable.

Thus in a Richmond paper[1] of 1831 may be found a poem, by Thomas Campbell, celebrating the revolutionary struggle of the Polish people. At this very moment, seventy-five miles away, yet unknown to the editor of this paper, there was then raging a revolt[2] of Negro slaves.

Here, in part, is what Campbell had to say about the Polish patriots:

'Tis freedom that calls you, though dim be the sun
The darkness around you dispelling,
Though death-fires enshroud you, and waste is begun,
She to deeds of high worth compelling,
Points to every loved altar and dwelling,
And demands from the sons of the noble in fame
If the hell-mark of slave must still blacken their name?

And this is the poem's ending:

The call of each sword upon Liberty's aid
Shall be written in gore on the steel of its blade!

But three days later this paper sings a very different tune. Those who have sought to remove the "hell-mark of slave" from their names are no longer "sons of the noble." They are banditti, monsters, blood-thirsty wolves, deluded wretches. Why? Firstly, of course, the steel of this blade is

---

1. Richmond (Virginia) *Enquirer*, August 23, 1831.
2. It is almost always referred to as an insurrection. The aim of an insurrection is not revolutionary; the aim of a rebellion is. A revolt is of less magnitude than a rebellion. See *Senate Document No. 209*, 57th Cong., 2d Sess. (Vol. 15) p. 258 note "Federal aid in domestic disturbances 1787-1903" prepared under direction of Maj.-Gen. H. C. Corbin by F. T. Wilson—Washington, 1903. Government Printing Office.

but 75 miles away, not 5500. However, the sword is wielded not for governmental reform; here the desire is, according to the leader,[3] that ".... the first should be last and the last should be first." But that is not all. This sword is raised by Negroes, by blacks, by those whom God very obviously put on this earth to serve and work for the white man. For that they were made, and only for that.[4] Thus they were slaves only in name, actually their condition represented "..... the mere external adaptation of natural law."[5] "And," exclaimed the eminent Professor Thomas R. Dew, "has it come at last to this: that the hellish plots and massacres of Dessalines, Gabriel, and Nat Turner, are to be compared to the noble deeds and devoted patriotism of Lafayette, Kosciusko, and Schrynecki?" To Thomas Dew the answer is a most emphatic no. The reason is that "To turn him [the Negro] loose in the manhood of his physical passions, but in the infancy of his uninstructed reason, would be to raise up a creature resembling the splendid fiction of a modern romance . . . ." i.e., Frankenstein's monster.[6]

---

3. *The Confessions of Nat Turner,* the leader of the late insurrection in Southampton, Va., as fully and voluntarily made to Thomas R. Gray, in the prison where he was confined, and acknowledged by him to be such when read before the Court of Southampton; with the certificate, under seal of the Court convened at Jerusalem, Nov. 5, 1831, for his trial. Also, an authentic account of the whole insurrection, with lists of the whites who were murdered, and of the negroes brought before the Court of Southampton, and there sentenced, etc. Baltimore: published by Thomas F. Gray, Lucas & Deaver, print. 1831. p. 11. See bibliography for discussion of this pamhlet. Hereafter it will be cited as *The Confessions.*

4. The idea of innate inferiority pervaded the pro-slavery argument. See, as examples, *The Pro-Slavery Argument;* as maintained by the most distinguished writers of the Southern States: Containing the several essays on the subject of Chancellor (William) Harper, Governor (J.H.) Hammond, Dr. (W.G.) Simms, and Professor (T.R.) Dew, Charleston, 1852.—passim; *Pro-Slavery Thought in the Old South* by William Sumner Jenkins, Chapel Hill, 1935, University of North Carolina Press—passim.

5. W. S. Jenkins, *op. cit.,* p. 252.

6. "Review of the debate in the Virginia legislature of 1831 and 1832" in *Pro-Slavery Argument, op. cit.,* pp. 448 and 450—in the latter Dew is quoting George Canning. This was first printed in pamphlet form by Thomas White in Richmond, 1832, and many times reprinted.

INTRODUCTION

In the anti-slavery debate of the Virginia legislature of 1831-1832, precipitated, as will be shown, by the Turner Revolt, Mr. William Preston directly stated[7] ". . . . if those who are slaves here, were not what they are; if, Mr. Speaker, they were white men in oppression and bondage, I would rejoice in a revolution here." Likewise, Harriet Martineau wrote[8] of a young slaveholder who admitted ". . . . that if it could be proved that negroes are more than a link between man and brute, the rest follows of course, and he must liberate all his."

This idea of the innate inferiority of the Negro people has afflicted most of the later writers on this event, and has, therefore, distorted their work. Thus W. S. Drewry, who time and again refers to Negroes as inferior people,[9] is compelled then to state[10] that only the deluded, the cowardly, and the stupid among the slaves ever took part in a revolt, although this contradicts his earlier description[11] of Nat Turner as ". . . . a man of considerable mental ability and wide information . . . ."

For a like reason R. R. Howison has great difficulty in accounting for the fact that, so far as the evidence shows, there was no instance of rape or attempted rape by the followers of Turner.[12] Howison is reduced to saying:[13] "Remembering the brutal passions of the negro, we can only account

---

7. Speech delivered in the House of Delegates, January 16, 1832, in Richmond *Enquirer*, February 9, 1832.
8. *Society in America*, by H. Martineau, in two volumes, fourth edition, New York and London, 1837. Saunders and Otley—Volume I, p. 371.
9. *The Southampton Insurrection* by William Sidney Drewry, Washington, 1900, pp. 154, 174, 184, 192, 194. This was also published, same place and date, as *Slave Insurrections in Virginia 1830-1865*.
10. *Ibid.*, pp. 63, 192.
11. *Ibid.*, p. 27.
12. *New York Evening Post*, September 5, 1831; "Nat Turner's Insurrection", by Thomas Wentworth Higginson in *Atlantic Monthly*, August, 1861, Vol. VIII, pp. 173-187, reprinted in his *Travellers and Outlaws*, Boston and New York, 1889. See p. 176 of article.
13. *A history of Virginia from its discovery . . . . to the present time* by Robert R. Howison, 2 vols. Richmond, New York, London, 1848, Vol. II, p. 444.

for this fact by supposing the actors to have been appalled by the very success of their hideous enterprise." Drewry,[14] on the other hand, while having no evidence to controvert this, states that women were insulted and offers further, without reference, some romantic nonsense about Turner offering to save a fair white damsel if she would but marry him. J. C. Ballagh[15] goes still further and writes, ". . . . . strange to say only a single well authenticated case of attempted violation of a female occurred." But, unfortunately, no authority is given.

Ballagh also writes[16] of the superstitions of the Negro revolutionists as something unique to such peoples and the ". . . . effect of even ordinary solar phenomena upon negro intelligence . . . ."—whatever the last two words may mean—when referring to the fact that Nat Turner accepted the eclipse of the sun of February 12, 1831, as a sign that the time had come to begin the revolt. But a contemporary paper[17] states: "A fanatic at New York preached, that during the eclipse the whole city South of Canal Street would sink. Some persons actually went to the upper part of the city." And Olmsted quotes[18] from a Charleston paper of 1855 to the effect that the majority of the poor whites of North Carolina were ". . . . totally given up to a species of hallucination . . . ." and that ". . . . nearly all believed implicitly in witchcraft . . . ." Does not Mark Sullivan state[19] that "In the 1920's the wife of President Harding used to consult a Washington astrologer?"

But if the viewpoint, to which the modern anatomist,

---

14. W. S. Drewry, *op. cit.*, p. 117.
15. *A History of Slavery in Virginia* by James Curtis Ballagh, John Hopkins Un. Studies in Historical and Political Science, Extra Volume XXIV, Baltimore, 1902, p. 93.
16. *Ibid.*, p. 94 note 92.
17. *The Liberator*, Boston, February 19, 1831—quoting the N.Y. *Patriot*.
18. Frederick Law Olmsted, *A Journey in the Seaboard Slave States.* . . . In two volumes, New York and London, 1904 (first issued in 1856) Vol. I, p. 389.
19. *Our Times* by Mark Sullivan, New York, 1926, Vol. I, p. 406, note 1.

anthropologist and psychologist point,[20] that no data exist to show the innate inferiority of the Negro (or any other peoples) but that, on the contrary, what data exist tend to confirm the opposite conclusion, succinctly expressed by Otto Klineberg:[21] "It is safe to say that as the environment of the Negro approximates more and more closely that of the White, his inferiority tends to disappear," then one need not find himself in the dilemma of acclaiming one man as a martyr because he is white, and calling another man a wretch because of some degree of coloration.

Specifically one may then, and should, consider the followers of Nat Turner not as deluded wretches and monsters (unless all revolutionists may thus be described) but rather as further examples of the woefully long, and indeed veritably endless, roll of human beings willing to resort to open struggle in order to get something precious to them—peace, prosperity, liberty, or, in a word, a greater amount of happiness.

---

20. As examples see—Franz Boas, *The Mind of Primitive Man*, New York, 1913, passim., and his *Anthropology and Modern Life*, New York, 1928, passim., Otto Klineberg, *Race Differences*, New York, 1935, passim.; E. B. Reuter, chapter on "Racial Differences" in his *The American Race Problem*, New York, 1927; *Race Relations* by W. D. Weatherford and C. S. Johnson, passim, New York, 1934; A. L. Kroeber, *Anthropology*, New York, 1923, esp. pp. 36-79; article by Franklin P. Hall in the *American Journal of Anatomy*, 1909, Vol. 9, pp. 1-32; H. C. Link on "What is intelligence?" in the *Atlantic Monthly* of September 1923; Robert S. Woodworth, *Psychology*, 3rd ed., New York, 1934, p. 79; W. O. Brown, *Journal of Negro History*, Vol. XVI, 1931, pp. 43-60. A brilliant application of this is W. E. B. Du Bois' *Black Reconstruction*, New York, 1935.
21. *Race Differences, op. cit.*, p. 189, O. Klineberg.

THE ENVIRONMENT

The Turner Revolt was the extra drop of water that overflows a cup, it was the precipitated pebble that causes ripples in a pond. And just as the effect of that one drop or that pebble would be nil, or almost indiscernible were there an empty cup or a dried-up pond, so the significance of the Revolt would have been very slight if it had not been true that it came at about the end of a decade of depression and some five or six years of intensive agitation among the slaves in this hemisphere. It is, then, important for a clearer understanding of this event to consider these two probably closely related factors which made up the vital setting.

A: Economic Depression

It is possible to point to the pictures of eastern Virginia drawn by Virginians (usually Western) in the debate of the House of Delegates of 1831-1832. They would be pictures[1] of "desolation and decay," of "stationary" towns and "declining" villages. But these descriptions are noteworthy for a lack of preciseness, and one's faith in them may further be lessened by realization of the fact that most of the artists had axes to grind. Yet, though we turn to facts and figures, and to the accounts of more disinterested and less rhetorical witnesses, the picture remains much the same.

---

1. Some of the speeches were issued in pamphlet form by Thomas White in Richmond, 1832. They are bound in one volume, *Virginia Slavery Debate of 1832*, in the Virginia State Library, Richmond. The quotations are from the speeches of W. H. Brodnax of Dinwiddie on Jan. 19 and Thomas Marshall of Fauquier on Jan. 14 and 20. Long extracts from these speeches are in *The Progress of Slavery in the United States* by G. M. Weston, Washington, 1857, pp. 200 ff and in *History of the Rise and Fall of the Slave Power in America*, by Henry Wilson, Boston, 1872, 2 vols., I, pp. 192 ff.

Thus Craven[2] points to the lamentations of Virginia papers in the 1820s. They referred to the fact that gentlemen farmers and fine dwellings had disappeared and: "In their places had come poorer homes, truck patches of cabbages and potatoes where once the great gardens of jassamines, tulips and roses grew, and families that knew not education or hospitality." It is at about this time that John Randolph writes[3] of "Poverty stalking through the land while we are engaged in political metaphysics. . . . ." The decade of the twenties was the period between the former high natural fertility of the soil and the future scientific methods of farming, which, together with the returned prosperity of the lower South and thus a greater market for Virginia slaves, were to cement the interests of the propertied classes of most of Virginia with the entire slave system.[4]

In an Alabama newspaper[5] of 1831 may be found this item: "The Cotton Market—The very low price of this great staple commodity of the southern country and the depressed condition of the market in every part of the world, furnish matter of anxious interest to the cultivator of the soil." In an appendix to an article by David Christy of Cincinnati this appears:[6] "Production and manufacture of cotton now

2. *Soil Exhaustion as a factor in the agricultural history of Virginia and Maryland 1606-1860* by Avery O. Craven, University of Illinois Studies in Social Sciences, Vol. XIII, No. 1 (1926), p. 126, Urbana, Illinois, see also 122; and *The Cotton Kingdom, a chronicle of the old South* by W. E. Dodd (Chronicles of America, ed. by A. Johnson, Vol. 27) New Haven, Toronto, London, 1919, p. 7 & 9; *History of Agriculture in the Southern United States to 1860* by L. C. Gray, assisted by E. K. Thompson, 2 vols. Washington, 1933. Vol 2, p. 666; *American Negro Slavery* . . . . by U. B. Phillips, New York, London, 1918. pp. 183, 213, 216.
3. Letter of Nov. 15, 1831 to Dr. Brockenbrough in *The Life of John Randolph of Roanoke* by H. A. Garland (2 vols.) complete in one volume, 11th edition, New York, 1857, Vol. II, p. 345.
4. A. O. Craven, *op. cit.*, 122; *Sectionalism in Virginia from 1776 to 1861* by C. H. Ambler, Chicago, 1910, p. 187.
5. *The Southern Advocate*, Huntsville, Alabama, Nov. 25, 1831.
6. "Cotton is King: or slavery in the light of political economy" in *Cotton is King, and pro-slavery arguments*, edited by K. N. Elliot, with articles by J. H. Hammond, W. Harper, D. Christy, T. Stringfellow, C. Hodge, A. T. Bledsoe and S. A. Cartwright and by the editor, Augusta, Ga., 1860, p. 252.

8

[1825] greatly above the consumption, and prices fell so as to produce general distress and stagnation, which continued with more or less intensity throughout 1828 and 1829. The fall of prices was about 55 per cent."

With the fall in the price of cotton went a very closely corresponding decline in the price of slaves, which spelt disaster to Virginia, the most important slave-market of this country. (The marketing of slaves was very important in making the slave system profitable to the slaveholders of eastern Virginia.[7]) This fact is clearly shown in the table prepared by U. B. Phillips.[8] Both cotton and slaves were the cheapest from 1825 to 1830 that they were to be until the one disappeared. The approximate price in Virginia of a prime field hand hit rock bottom ($400) in 1825 and stayed there until 1829. Not until 1836 was the money value of a slave as great as it had been in 1819, but the uptrend started in 1830. About one year later the uptrend in cotton prices had also definitely started.

B: POPULATION DISPROPORTION

As already indicated, the piling up of Negroes in the tidewater counties was an indication of economic maladjustment. Virginia supplied the lower South with slaves. A depression in the lower South meant less of a demand for slaves. A lowered demand meant a lowered price and a clogging of the market, i.e., an increase in the slave population. This was what happened in the ten years preceding the Turner Revolt.

---

7. W. E. Dodd, *The Cotton Kingdom* ". . . . most profitable product was the slave who could be sold." p. 7, *op. cit.*, also pp. 9, 80 and 51. Speech of Thomas J. Randolph of Albemarle on Jan. 21, 1832 in House of Delegates—Thomas White, Richmond, 1832, p. 15; Also *Sectionalism and Representation in South Carolina* by W. A. Schaper, American Historical Association, 1900 (1), p. 388.
8. U. B. Phillips, *American Negro Slavery, op. cit.*, opposite page 370 and in same author's *Life and Labor in the Old South*, students edition, Boston, 1931, p. 177.

The data support this generalization but a precise soul would be driven to distraction by these same data, for disagreement in detail is their distinguishing feature. But the figures are, usually, close enough to satisfy any but the most precise; surely close enough to make valid certain generalizations.

The figures, in a few different kinds of sources, for Virginia as a whole reveal for the two decades, 1810-1820, 1820-1830, a slow but steady growth in the three classifications of population.

a) Population changes in Virginia as a whole 1810-1830.[9]

	1810			1820		
	White	Slave	Free Negro	White	Slave	Free Negro
ABDY	None Given			None Given		
ADAMS	551534	392518	30570	603074	425153	36889
CONVENTION	551553	392456	30570	603381	425148	36875
NILES	551534	392518	30570	603324	425153	36889

	1830		
ABDY	694445	469724	47031
ADAMS	694300	469757	47348
CONVENTION	694302	469755	47349
NILES	694440	469715	47086

But when these figures are allotted according to geographic sections, it becomes easier to understand why the Turner Revolt had, in Virginia, the effects it did. It helps one to understand the uneasy condition of society directly preceding the episode, which will later be discussed in detail, and the debates, bills, letters, laws, migrations, terror

9. Abdy, E. S., *Journal of a residence and tour in the United States....* London, 1835, in 3 volumes, Vol. II, p. 203n. Adams, A. D., *The Neglected Period of Anti-Slavery Agitation in America (1808-1831)*, Boston and London, 1907, pp. 3, 4, 5, 6, 7. *Documents containing statistics of Virginia ordered to be printed* by the State Convention sitting in the City of Richmond, 1850-51. Richmond 1851. No pagination—calculated from figures given under tables beginning "The Census"—A Tabular statement . . . ." *Niles' Weekly Register*, Vol. XL p. 261-262, June 11, 1831, Baltimore.

and ideological changes which, after the Revolt swept Virginia and, soon thereafter, the rest of the South. The salient factors in these figures are the low rate of increase of the white population in eastern Virginia and the higher rate of increase of the Negroes therein from, especially, 1820-1830, with the reverse being true in Western Virginia.

The errors concerning these figures are serious. First, Niles[10] gives two sets of figures, both of which agree quite closely with the official data, as far as Western Virginia is concerned, but the first of which is completely wrong as far as eastern Virginia is concerned. The most significant error here is his figure for Whites in Tidewater Virginia for 1830, 158,523, which is 100 less than the same region had in 1820. His second set of figures gives this item as 166,089 which is fairly close to the official figure of 167,001.[11] And, what aggravates the case, Niles, in discussing the figures, uses the first set, the wrong set, and thus states ". . . . the Tidewater counties have actually decreased in their White inhabitants . . . ."[12] A. O. Craven[13] makes the same kind of an error, but the magnitude of his is greater than that of Niles. Craven says: "From 1820 to 1830 Virginia's rate of population increase fell from 37½ per cent where it had stood in the previous decade, to 13½ per cent. The increase of free whites fell from 35 per cent to 15 per cent for the state as a whole with a loss of 92,625 persons in the eastern section." (Craven's references for this are "United States Census; Farmer's (sic) Register, I, 5.") He goes on: "The total increase of whites in the next period (1830-1840) was only a trifle over 3 per cent and there were some 26,000 fewer people in the older portions of the state in 1840 than there had been ten years earlier. Many counties in the Tidewater and Piedmont regions lost population and only the growth of the western

10. *Niles' Weekly Register*, XL, *op. cit.*, 261.
11. *Documents ordered . . . . by Convention of 1850-51, op. cit.*, same table.
12. *Niles' Weekly Register*, XL, *op. cit.*, p. 262.
13. Avery O. Craven, *Soil exhaustion etc. op. cit.*, p. 123.

11

counties gave the state any gain whatsoever." And the reference here is "Farmer's (sic) Register, I, 40."

The census figures will shortly be given. They disagree with those cited by Craven, and Craven, it is believed, misread Edmund Ruffin's journal also. The same percentage figures are there given, but the first, 37½, does not apply to the decade 1810-1820, but from 1790-1800. Where Craven got the figure 92,625 is not known. What the source he cites says is ". . . . while, in 1790, there was in that district (Eastern Virginia) a majority of 25,000 whites, the slave and free colored population outnumbered them at every successive census, until, 1830, the excess was upward of 81,000."[14] The second series of statements made by Craven is also in error. The reference to a periodical of 1834 cannot, of course, substantiate Craven's statement concerning population trends from 1830-1840. Where that was gotten from is not known. It does not agree with the official figures. The source mentioned to substantiate his ideas about population changes in counties does not do so. It is there[15] simply stated, and not quite accurately, that some eastern counties lost in whites from 1820-1830, but nowhere is it said that ". . . . only the growth of the western counties gave the state any gain whatsoever."

The facts concerning population in Virginia as given by the official publication of that state, based upon census returns, are:

b) *Sectional population changes, Virginia 1810-1840*[16]

(District 1 includes the counties from the sea coast to the Tidewater; district 2 the counties from the head of the Tidewater to the Blue Ridge Mountains—commonly called

---

14. *The Farmers' Register* . . . . Shellbank, Va., Vol. I, P. S. 1834.
15. *Farmers' Register*, I, 40, gives 14 eastern counties as losing whites; actually 15 did, as shown in source this note.
16. *Documents* . . . . *Convention 1850-51, op. cit.*, see pages beginning "The Census—A Tabular statement of the free whites, free colored, and total population in each county . . . . according to the census of 1790, 1800, 1810, '20, '30, '40, '50."

The Enviorment

the Piedmont; district 3 the counties between the Blue
Ridge and the Allegheny Mountains, commonly called the
Valley; district 4 the counties West of the Allegheny Moun-
tains.)

1810

District	White	Slave	Free Negro
1	153271	174298	19421
2	185556	185349	7874
3	108355	23708	2552
4	104371	9101	723

1820

1	161687	176496	23077
2	187486	205501	9501
3	121096	29785	3275
4	133552	13366	1022

1830

1	167001	185457	28980
2	208656	230861	12026
3	134791	34772	4745
4	183854	18665	1598

1840

1	170530	172791	29262
2	198868	222460	13031
3	136796	33697	5188
4	234774	20040	2360

Percentages will display the trend more clearly:

c) Population change by percentage and districts, Virginia, 1810-1840.[17] (1830-1840 is added for comparison and
will be further used later.)

	DISTRICT ONE			DISTRICT TWO		
	White	Slave	Free Negro	White	Slave	Free Negro
1810-20	5.4%	1.2%	18.7%	1.0%	10.8%	20.6%
1820-30	3.2	5.0	25.5	11.2	12.3	26.5
1830-40	2.0	−6.8	7.4	−4.7	−3.5	8.3
	DISTRICT THREE			DISTRICT FOUR		
1810-20	11.7	25.6	28.3	27.5%	46.8%	41.3%
1820-30	11.3	16.7	44.8	38.1	39.4	56.3
1830-40	1.4	−3.0	9.3	27.7	7.3	47.7

17. *Ibid.*, percentages calculated, except those for 1830-1840 which are
given in source.

13

	EASTERN VIRGINIA (Dist. 1 and 2)			WESTERN VIRGINIA (Dist. 3 and 4)		
1810-20	3.0%	6.2%	19.3%	19.5%	30.5%	31.2%
1820-30	7.5	8.9	20.5	25.3	23.8	47.6
1830-40	−1.6	−5.0	3.3	16.6	0.5	18.8

It appears, then, that as to the quality of the trend Niles and Craven were right but both exaggerated, the latter more than the former, its quantity.

C: SOUTHAMPTON COUNTY ITSELF

To make more complete the picture of the economic environment surrounding the Turner Revolt, it is necessary to examine Southampton County, the precise scene of its occurrence. The first thing to observe is that it is located in the southeastern part of Virginia, in the Tidewater section, bordering on the State of North Carolina. It is, further, important to realize that Southampton was an important economic unit within the Tidewater area. Its size is 600 square miles. In 1840 it was the leading county in the number of swine, in cotton produced and products of the orchard. It was second in potatoes and in rice.[18] In 1830, out of 39 Tidewater counties, only three surpassed Southampton in its number of free Negroes, and only four in its number of whites and its number of slaves.[19]

Since it was one of the Tidewater counties, one expects it to show signs of the economic decay prevalent for some dozen years preceding 1831. The following table will illustrate both this decay and the relative economic position of the county:

d) *Economic position of Southampton County, 1810-30.*[20] (In 1810 there were 104 counties, in 1820 there were 110 and in 1830 there were 111 in Virginia.)

---

18. *A History of Virginia from its discovery and settlement by Europeans to the present time* by R. R. Howison, 2 Vols. New York and London, 1848. Vol. II, pp. 498-500.
19. See first group of tables in *Documents . . . . Convention. 1850-1851, op. cit.*
20. *Ibid.,* see table number 4 in "A statement shewing the amount of taxes assessed for each county, City and Town, for the years 1790, 1800, 1810, '20, '30 and '40. . . ."

	1810	1820	1830
Tax on Land and Lots	$2722.16	$2207.20	$1468.84
Rank	fifth	forty-fifth	forty-sixth
Tax on Slaves	$1604.68	$2813.30	$1454.95
Rank	sixteenth	twenty-seventh	eighteenth

The population changes in this county for these twenty years reflect the same disturbing trend as those for the eastern section as a whole: That is, the rates of growth of the slave population, and of the free Negroes were considerably faster than that of the white population. It may here be noted that according to Drewry,[21] there were "numerous Quakers" in the county. He gives no reference and no figures on this have been seen.

e) Population changes, Southampton County, 1810-30.[22]

	Whites	Growth Rate	Free Negro	Rate	Slaves	Rate	Total	Rate
1810	5982	——	1109	——	6406	——	13,497	——
1820	6127	2.4%	1306	17.7%	6737	5.1%	14,170	4.9%
1830	6573	7.2	1745	33.6	7756	15.1	16,074	13.4

Moreover, directly prior to the Turner Revolt there had occurred a series of events which were more stirring, more mass-awakening, than soil exhaustion, or price decline, or disproportionate population growth. The latter were, in-

---

21. *The Southampton Insurrection* by W. S. Drewry, Washington, 1900, p. 108. Also mentioned by reviewer of this book in *The Virginia Magazine of History and Biography*, Richmond, Volume 8, No. 1, July 1900, p. 222.

22. There is unusual agreement on these figures. They are so given in the first group of tables of the *Documents . . . of the Convention of 1850-1851*, *op. cit.*, *Niles' Weekly Register*, Vol. XLIII, p. 30, Sept. 8, 1832; *The Southampton Insurrection* by W. S. Drewry, p. 108 note 3; *The American Annual Register* 1830-31, Boston & N.Y., 1832, p. 381. But J. H. Hinton, S. L. Knapp & J. O. Choules, *The History and Topography of the United States of North America*, (2 Vols, 2nd edition) Boston, 1846, Vol. II, p. 443 gives the total, 1830, as 16073 and the slaves as 7755 which is what S. B. Weeks, "The Slave Insurrection in Virginia, 1831, known as Old Nat's War" in *Magazine of American History*, Vol. XXV, No. 6, June 1891 pp. 448-458 does—see p. 454 n.

deed, the main figures in the picture, but there were significant minor features, shadows and colorings. There were evidences of slave unrest, both here and in foreign lands, there were anti-slavery pamphlets, letters, petitions and speeches, repressive legislative efforts, Negro conventions, the beginnings of Garrisonianism. These must be shown to complete the setting for the event under consideration.

D: BRITAIN AND LATIN AMERICA

With the growth of industrial capitalism in the first half of the nineteenth century went a growth in the democratic movement. Both these developments were very prominent in England and the increasing agitation over slavery in her colonies is one manifestation of the progressive spirit of the times.[23] There is evidence that some members of the West Indian slave-holding group considered slave labor of doubtful economic utility. Niles,[24] in 1829, tells of a petition from the coffee growers of Dominica (a small island now part of the Leeward Islands, about 25 miles from Martinique) to Parliament praying that they be permitted to export all their slaves. This project was vehemently denounced by the sugar planters of the same island. Niles goes on to point out that while in 1812 there were 27,000 slaves in Dominica, on December 31, 1828 there were but 12,200. Furthermore, staple crop producers within British India, where slavery was forbidden, petitioned Parliament to abolish slavery in the West Indies. And it was in the decade of the twenties that "Exhaustion of the soil and the competition of foreign sugar from Cuba and Brazil were depressing their (the British West Indian slaveholders') one staple industry. . . . .[25]

---

23. S. E. Morison says this concerning abolitionism here, at this time, but offers no explanation of the progressive spirit. *The Life and Letters of Harrison Gray Otis* . . . . 2 Vols, Boston and N.Y. 1913, Vol. II, p. 256.
24. *Niles' Weekly Register*, Vol. XXXVI, p. 114, April 18, 1829.
25. R. Coupland, *The British Anti-Slavery Movement*, London, 1933, p. 123.

The abolition movement in England grew not only because it fitted the *Zeitgeist*, and appears to have been supported by some economic groups, but also because from 1829 to 1832, there were numerous, and, at times, serious slave uprisings or plots within some of the British West Indies, and in Martinique, Santiago (then called St. Jago) and Brazil.[26]

The first island, apparently, in which a slave uprising at this period occurred was Martinique.[27] A little later, report is made of an uprising in Antigua and then in St. Jago[28] (Santiago). Next is a report of an outbreak in Caracas (Venezuela) starting on May 11, 1831 and some months later of the start of a revolt in Jamaica.[29] From the contemporary reports it appears likely that the plots in Tortola and Brazil occurred a short time after the Turner Revolt.[30]

Whether these revolts, economic facts and the general progressive spirit are the explanations of the revivified abolitionist propaganda in England or not, the fact, and for this discussion, the important fact, remains that the propaganda was vitalized and it did have its repercussions in this country. According to one contemporary English writer,[31] the change in the abolitionist movement was qualitative as well

26. T. W. Higginson states that these revolts followed "by some secret sympathy" the Turner Revolt, *Atlantic Monthly*, Aug. 1861, Vol. 8, p. 173. Also in S. B. Weeks, *Magazine of American History*, *op. cit.*, p. 456. W. S. Drewry, *The Southampton Insurrection*, Washington, 1900, seems to imply the same, p. 152. As a matter of fact, most of these revolts preceded Turner's.

27. *The Liberator* (Boston) March 12, 1831, Vol. I, p. 43 (also March 26, 1831) *Niles' Weekly Register* (Baltimore) XL, 52, March 19, 1831.

28. *The Liberator*, Vol. I, pp. 71, 74, 90, Apr. 30, May 7, June 4, 1831.

29. *Ibid.*, Vol. I, p. 151, Sept. 17, 1831; p. 155, Sept. 24, quoting the Bermuda *Royal Gazette* of August 9, 1831.

30. *Niles' Weekly Register*, XLI, Oct. 15, 1831, p. 131; *The Liberator*, Vol. I, p. 167, Oct. 15, 1831; Oct. 22, 1831, p. 170. W. S. Drewry, *The Southampton Insurrection*, *op. cit.*, p. 152 mentions a revolt in Tortugas, now part of the Cayman Islands. No reference is given and no further evidence of this has been seen. He does not mention Tortola—perhaps he confused the two.

31. G. W. Alexander, *Letters on the slave-trade, slavery and emancipation*. . . . London, 1842, pp. 22-23.

as quantitative in 1830, moving to a demand for immediate emancipation. G. H. Barnes[32] writes: "In the nation as a whole, however, the progress of the [British Anti-Slavery] movement was noticed only in a small way before 1830; but the parliamentary debates in August of that year put it on the front page of the great daily newspapers. Everywhere men were asking what it signified for America. . . . . With interest painful or exultant, Americans followed the struggle in parliament and the agitation in the empire." On January 10, 1831, John Quincy Adams[33] wrote "The abolition of slavery will pass like a pestilence over all the British Colonies in the West Indies; it may prove an earthquake upon this continent."

Some events in Spanish America also help one to understand the "peculiarly sensitive" condition of the slaveholders.[34] It is true, of course, that the anti-slavery law, promulgated by Mexico in 1829, was evaded by American slaveholders resident in Texas,[35] who now called their slaves apprentices. But, as Miss Martineau stated:[36] "The Mexicans took alarm; decreed in the State Legislature of Texas that no apprenticeship should, on any pretense, be for a longer term than ten years; forbade further immigration from the United States; and sent a small body of troops to enforce

32. Gilbert H. Barnes, *The Anti-slavery impulse 1830-1844*, American Historical Association, N.Y. and London, 1933, p. 29.
33. *Memoirs of John Quincy Adams* . . . . edited by C. F. Adams, Phila., 1876, Vol. VIII, 269, quoted, in part by G. H. Barnes, *op. cit.*, 29, See also *The Life, Travels and opinions of Benjamin Lundy* . . . . compiled . . . behalf of his children—p. 242. (See bibliography for note on this), Philadelphia, 1847.
34. The quoted words are from J. Macy, *The Anti-Slavery Crusade* . . . New Haven, Toronto, London, 1921 (Vol. 28 of *Chronicles of America*, A. Johnson, ed.) p. 61.
35. J. F. Rhodes, *History of United States from the Compromise* of 1850, N.Y., 1896, Vol. I, p. 76.
36. Harriet Martineau, *Society in America*, 4th edition, N.Y. & London, 1837, 2 vols. Vol I, p. 326; see also *Life of Henry Clay* by Carl Schurz, 2 Vols. Vol. II, pp. 88-89. (American Statesmen, edited by J. T. Morse, Jr.) Boston and New York, 1890; Marquis James, *The Raven, a biography of Sam Houston*, New York, 1929, pp. 181-182. W. S. Drewry, *The Southampton Insurrection, op. cit.*, p. 130.

the prohibition. This was in 1829 and 1830." True, soon Mexico itself exempted Texas from the abolition law, and within seven years the sovereignty of Texas was recognized and the problem satisfactorily resolved for the slaveholders. But in 1830 it was a problem and it did cause uneasiness. The attempt of Mexico, and Colombia, apparently backed by England and France, to get rid of slavery and Spanish rule in Cuba and Puerto Rico, starting in the late 1820s, was another source of concern for the American slaveholder at this same period.[37]

E: STIRRINGS IN THE SOUTH

There were, too, in the years directly preceding the Turner Revolt, events at home of a very disturbing nature.

Governor John Floyd of Virginia, in his message to the Legislature of 1829-1830, stated: "A spirit of dissatisfaction and insubordination was manifested by the slaves in different parts of the country from this place [Richmond] to the seaboard."[38] The newspapers of the south, and, indeed, of the rest of the country were exceedingly stingy in allotting space to such news.[39] But the following item[40] indicates, if not actual disturbances among the Virginia Negroes, certainly fear of this: "On Saturday, last week, before the court of Hastings at Richmond, came on the trial of Jasper Ellis, a colored man charged with the design of promoting an insur-

---

37. "Henry Clay" by T. E. Burton in *The American Secretaries of State and their diplomacy*, S. F. Bemis, editor, New York, 1928, Vol. IV, pp. 134, 143; J. Macy, *The Anti-Slavery Crusade, op. cit.*, p. 61; W. S. Drewry, *The Southampton Insurrection*, Washington, 1900, pp. 126-127.

38. *Journal of the House of Delegates*, 1829-30, Richmond, 1830, p. 8; quoted by T. M. Whitfield, *Slavery Agitation in Virginia 1829-1832*, J. Hopkins Un. Studies . . . Extra volumes, new series, No. 10, Baltimore, 1930, p. 54.

39. *Niles' Weekly Register*, Vol. XLI, p. 74 (Oct. 1, 1831); p. 221 (Nov. 19, 1831); H. Martineau, *Society in America, op. cit.*, Vol. I, pp. 109-110; C. H. Ambler, *Thomas Ritchie, a study in Virginia Politics*, Richmond, 1913, p. 25.

40. *Niles' Weekly Register*, XXXVII, p. 39, (Sept. 12, 1829).

Nat Turner's slave Rebellion
NAT TURNER'S SLAVE REBELLION
Nat Turner's slave Rebellion

rection of the slaves, about the beginning of August. A wit-
ness related the conversation which he had overheard
between Ellis and another colored man, relative to the supposed rising of the blacks. The case was submitted to the
court without argument, when the prisoner was acquitted."

The evidence concerning North Carolina is more full. In
the excitement following the Turner Revolt a question kept
recurring to the minds of the newspaper editors: Who were
these Negroes? And, once, the Richmond *Enquirer*[41] asked:
"Were they connected with the desperadoes who harrassed
(sic) N. Carolina last year?" The items in the *Liberator* are
revealing.[42] "Many inhabitants of Rutherford Co. N.C. are
in pursuit of a black outlaw, Big George, who with two females, has committed many robberies for some time past.
Bloodhounds have tracked them, and one was lately struck
and driven back by them. They were lately shot at by a
party of eight men, but escaped." A week later, the *Liberator,* quoted the "Roanoke Adv." as follows:[43] "Milton (N.C.)
Dec. 25. We have learned from authority of the most un-
doubted kind, that the inhabitants of Newbern, Tarborough,
Hillsborough, and their vicinities, are considerably excited,
with the anticipation of insurrectional movements among
their slaves. Our informant, just from the latter place, states
that considerable consternation exists among its citizens:
that they have provided arms and ammunition, and are vig-
ilantly patrolling every exposed position. The inhabitants
of Newbern being advised of the assemblage of sixty armed
slaves in a swamp in their vicinity, the military were called
out, and surrounding the swamp, *killed the whole party.* It
appears from various rumors that Christmas morning had
been selected as the period of rebellious motions." Two
months later Garrison gives[44] an extract of a letter to the

---

41. Richmond *Enquirer,* August 30, 1831.
42. The *Liberator* (Boston), Vol. I, p. 7, January 8, 1831. (emphasis in original).
43. *Ibid.,* Vol. I, p. 11, Jan. 15, 1831. (emphasis in original).
44. The *Liberator,* Vol. I, p. 47, March 19, 1831 (emphasis by Garrison).

editors of the New York *Sentinel,* dated Washington, N.C. January 7. It states: "There has been much shooting of negroes in this neighborhood recently, in consequence of *symptoms of liberty* having been discovered among them. These inhuman acts are kept profoundly secret—wherefore I know not. Two companies of troops have very lately been stationed here."

Another news item from a contemporary[45] periodical indicates that similar events were occurring in Kentucky at this time: "Four negroes were executed at Greenup, Ky. for a murder committed on their owner, while he was transporting them down the Ohio to the New Orleans market. They died with astonishing firmness, without shewing the least compunction for the crime committed, and one of them, the instant before he was launched from the cart, exclaimed —'death—death at any time in preference to slavery.' "

The data pertaining to the stirrings in Louisiana are greater and point to a more widespread movement——or, what is quite as important, to the belief on the part of the whites that there was such a movement——than in any of the other states, excepting, perhaps, North Carolina. Niles[46] reported: "Louisiana. There has been a rising of the slaves on certain plantations about 40 miles from New Orleans, 'up the coast.' It created a general alarm, but was speedily suppressed, and two of the ringleaders hung." About a year later he reports a "supposed plot" in New Orleans and states that, again, two Negroes were executed.[47] Here reference is also made to the discovery of the pamphlet "by the colored dealer in old clothes" (David Walker) of which more will soon be said. Garrison[48] refers to a plot at Plaquemines, a parish south of New Orleans, being discovered in October, 1830 and embracing one hundred Negroes, including some who were free.

---

45. *Niles' Weekly Register,* Vol. XXXVII, p. 277, Dec. 26, 1829.
46. *Ibid.,* Vol. XXXVI, p. 53, March 21, 1829.
47. *Ibid.,* Vol. XXXVIII, p. 157, April 24, 1830.
48. The *Liberator,* Vol. I, p. 3, January 1, 1831.

Drewry[49] refers to uneasiness among the slaves of Delaware and Maryland, which he ascribes to the activities of slave dealers. He offers no authority for this supposed causation and does not make clear when this unrest was noticed. He quotes a letter from the Baltimore *Patriot* on the trouble in Maryland, but does not give its date. In a government document[50] of 1903, however, it is stated that this unrest was observed in the Spring of 1831, that is, before the Turner Revolt. For this reason, and because it substantiates what has been said about other states, the passage is given in full: "The year 1831 was one of unusual uneasiness throughout the slave-holding section of the country, consequent upon an apprehended uprising of the negroes. Early in the spring of that year strong and urgent representations were made to the War Department by the authorities of Louisiana that a revolt was threatened by the slaves, and that the presence of a military force in New Orleans was necessary to the preservation of order and to allay the apprehensions of the people. To quiet these fears two companies of infantrymen were sent to that city and orders were given to neighboring posts to hold the troops in readiness for any emergency. Later in the season similar reports of disorderly conduct upon the part of the slaves came from Delaware, Maryland, Virginia and the Carolinas, and in order that a disposable force might be available to afford protection to such parts of the country as might require it, the garrison at Fort Monroe (Virginia) was augmented by five companies drawn from the northern seaboard."

F: ANTI-SLAVERY DEVELOPMENTS

The trend toward a less gradualistic and more vehement anti-slavery literature started a little more than one year

---

49. W. S. Drewry, The Southampton Insurrection, *op. cit.*, p. 152.
50. "Federal Aid in Domestic Disturbances 1787-1903" prepared under direction of Maj.-Gen. W. C. Corbin by F. T. Wilson, *Senate Document No. 209, 57th Cong., 2d sess.* (Vol. 15) p. 56 Washington, 1903. This source is referred to by A. B. Hart, *Slavery and Abolition 1831-1841* (Vol. 16 of The American Nation) New York, 1906.

before the Turner Revolt. The shift from one ideology to
another will be followed in greater detail later. Here it suf-
fices to point out that in the middle twenties the efforts of a
Frances Wright or of a Benjamin Lundy to lead the slaves
very gradually to emancipation and to put through an extensive colonization plan are allowed to go on.[51] Similarly, in
1826, a Virginia newspaper would publish the anti-slavery
views of an eminent lawyer, William Maxwell.[52] But in 1829
and 1830 appear the uncompromising David Walker[53] justify-
ing and vindicating the use of force for abolition and, on
January 1, 1831, the more pacifistic, but no less uncompromising writings of William Lloyd Garrison.

The Negro Convention,[54] which was first assembled at
Philadelphia on September 15, 1830 and transacted its business at its second meeting on June 6-11, 1831, is another
indication of the changed atmosphere in the years just preceding the Turner Revolt. This meeting was woefully neglected by the contemporary "respectable" press and has,
apparently, almost been forgotten by later writers. It was
publicly held and well attended and was addressed by some
of the leaders in the abolitionist movement, including Garrison, himself. It went on record as opposing the American
Colonization Society, but favoring Canadian colonization
work. It was here, too, that it was decided to attempt to

---

51. W. R. Waterman, *Frances Wright,* Columbia Un. Studies in history,
    economics and public law, CXV, No. 1, New York, 1924, p. 94 ff;
    The Life, Travels and Opinions of Benjamin Lundy, including his
    journeys to Texas and Mexico; with a sketch of contemporary events
    . . . . compiled under the direction and on behalf of his children,
    Philadelphia, 1847, pp. 206 ff. There is no adequate biography of
    Lundy.
52. A. D. Adams, *The Neglected Period of Anti-Slavery Agitation in
    America, 1808-1831,* Boston and London, 1908, p. 41.
53. (David) *Walker's Appeal,* in four articles; together with a preamble
    to the colored citizens of the world . . . Boston . . . Third edition,
    1830.
54. J. W. Cromwell, *The Negro in American History.* . . . Washington,
    1914, pp. 29 ff.; The *Liberator,* (Boston), October 22, 1831; W. E. B.
    DuBois in *John Brown* (American Crisis Biographies, E. P. Ober-
    holtzer, editor), Philadelphia, 1909, p. 86 mistakenly puts this Con-
    vention after the Turner Revolt.

establish a school, called a college, for Negroes in New Haven, Connecticut, which due to the opposition of the "best people," of that civilized community, including the Mayor himself, could not even be started.[55]

The economic and sociological phenomena that have been presented in the preceding pages caused political activity important in itself, and still more important because it helped bring the slavery question to a critical stage.

There was, within the State of Virginia, itself, the Constitutional Convention of 1829-1830 which has been exhaustively worked over in numerous works.[56] It has been shown that this was a vain struggle on the part of the West to introduce greater democracy, as direct election of the Governor, and, especially, to base representation and suffrage on population, not property (i.e., slaves). The population figures given earlier in this volume and the works cited explain this sectional cleavage, but here it is important to note that the anti-slavery sentiment of the Western members, which a year later the sword was to evoke very audibly, is observable and, as it were, rumbling under the surface.

But three weeks after the first meeting of the Convention (October 5) the Richmond *Enquirer*[57] printed the fears of the editor of the Charleston (S.C.) *Mercury*: "Already do the advocates of abolition rejoice even at the agitation of the subject and confidently predict the day of triumph. Sec-

---

55. *Niles' Weekly Register,* XLI, 88 October 1, 1831; H. Wilson, *History of the rise and fall of the slave power in America,* Boston, 1872, Volume I, 238-239.

56. As examples see, A. D. Adams, *The Neglected Period of Anti-Slavery Agitation . . . . op. cit.,* 54; C. H. Ambler, *Sectionalism in Virginia from 1776 to 1861,* Chicago, 1910, pp. 141 ff.; J. A. C. Chandler, *Representation in Virginia,* J. Hopkins Un. Studies in historical and political science, Baltimore, 1896, (No. 14), pp. 32-44; T. M. Whitfield, *Slavery Agitation in Virginia 1829-1832,* J. Hopkins Studies, New series, No. 10, Baltimore, 1930, p. 43; H. H. Simms, *The Rise of the Whigs in Virginia 1824-1840,* Richmond, 1929, pp. 36-39; H. A. Garland, *The Life of John Randolph of Roanoke,* 11th edition, N. Y. 1857, Vol. II, pp. 324-332.

57. Richmond *Enquirer,* October 27, 1829, quoted by C. H. Ambler, *Sectionalism,* op. cit., p. 146.

tional interests may clash, local jealousies may jar; eastern
and western Virginia may contend warmly and even fearfully, but we have no apprehension for the result." As a
matter of fact, of course, abolition was never even broached,
and Miss Adams appears correct in saying,[58] ". . . . . it seems
not at all a contest for or against slavery per se, but a jealous
rivalry of the West and the East. . . . ."

Yet the democratic principles of the Western delegates
involved them, often unwillingly, in abolitionist language.
Thus, Mr. Cooke, of Frederick County (Valley district)
while disclaiming advocacy of Negro freedom, in urging an
extended suffrage and representative base, said,[59] ". . . . that
no one man comes in the world with a mark on him, to
designate him as possessing superior rights to any other man;
that neither God nor nature recognize, in anticipation, the
distinctions of bond and free, of despot and slave; but that
these distinctions are artificial; are the work of man; are
the result of fraud and violence."

Disclaim abolitionist sentiments as the propounders of
these ideas usually did, the ideas were very annoying to the
delegates from the slave districts. Thus, Mr. P. P. Barbour
of Orange (Piedmont) said,[60] concerning the Bill of Rights,
". . . . if you give to the language, all the force which the
words literally import, (and they are, I believe, but an echo
of those in the Declaration of Independence) what will they
amount to, but a declaration of universal emancipation, to
a class of our population, not far short of a moiety of our
entire number, now in a state of slavery?" And Mr. John
Randolph (representing Charlotte County) declared: "There
is nothing which so alarms me, as to see the existence of the
fanatical spirit on this subject of negro slavery, as it is called,
growing up in the land."[61]

58. A. D. Adams, *The Neglected Period* . . . . *op. cit.*, p. 54.
59. Speech of October 27, 1829, *Proceedings and debates of the Vir-
    ginia State Convention of 1829-1830*. . . . Richmond, 1830, p. 55.
60. Speech of October 29, 1829, *Ibid.*, p. 91.
61. Speech of January 12, 1830, *Proceedings* . . . . *of* . . . . *Convention*,
    op. cit., p. 858.

There was, however, but one request aiming at the abolition of slavery. Certainly there was nothing of a fanatical spirit about it. This was a memorial (whether received and considered or not is not known) from Augusta County (Valley) ". . . . praying for the adoption of some provisions in the new constitution by which the slave population in the state may be checked, or reduced, and, if possible, ultimately done away with." Slavery is declared degrading and unprofitable and, further, it is feared that ". . . . those who remain seem destined to become martyrs to their love of Virginia, exposed to foreign enemies, to civil feuds, and to domestic insurrections, without the physical ability indispensable to their own preservation."[62]

Drewry[63] asserts that "The calling of a Constitutional Convention . . . . inspired in the slaves of Matthews, Isle of Wight, and the neighboring counties hopes of emancipation, and in case of failure of such declaration a determination to rebel and massacre the whites." He states, too, that the failure of the Convention to aid the Negroes is what convinced Nat Turner that it was time ". . . . to carry out his threats." Unfortunately, the writer does not explain how he obtained this information and his unsupported statement is not sufficient evidence. The evidence available permits one to point to the Convention proceedings as further indication of the unique feature of Virginian and southern life at this time—extreme uneasiness, doubt, fear, concerning the slavery issue. Certainly those features of the Convention alluded to *may* have aroused "hopes of emancipation" and chagrin at their being dashed, but whether they did or not is unknown.

There were three other political actions in Virginia, during this period, which are significant. In the 1830 legislature a Bill was introduced outlawing seditious writing (the immediate occasion was the Walker pamphlet) and pronounc-

---

62. *Niles' Weekly Register*, (Baltimore) XXXVI, July 25, 1829, p. 345.
63. W. S. Drewry, *The Southampton Insurrection*, Washington, 1900, p. 116.

ing illegal the meeting of free Negroes for purposes of instruction, with a penalty of 20 lashes for the Negro and $100 fine for any white involved. A slave owner who established a school for his slaves was to be fined not less than $50 nor more than $500. But while this passed the House 81 to 80, it was rejected in the Senate,[64] 11-7. The Walker pamphlet also caused Governor Floyd[65] of Virginia (and the Mayor of Savannah, Georgia) to write to the Mayor of Boston, Harrison Gray Otis, to inform him of the publication within his city of a seditious pamphlet and to request him to do what he could to suppress it, which was nothing.

G: NEW REPRESSIVE LEGISLATION

On April 7, 1831, the Virginia legislature passed a law which considerably, and adversely, affected the Negro population. Free Negroes remaining contrary to law were to be sold into slavery, and "all meetings of free negroes or mulattoes, at any school-house, church, meeting house or other place for teaching them reading or writing, either in the day or night, under whatsoever pretext, shall be deemed and considered as an unlawful assembly;" punishable by not more than 20 lashes for the Negroes and a fine of $50 for the whites present, whom the court might also send to jail for two months. It was further provided that any white person who, for pay, assembled with slaves in order to instruct them in reading and writing was to be fined not more than $100 and not less than $10. This act took effect on June 1, 1831.[66]

---

64. *Niles' Weekly Register*, XXXVIII, p. 88, March 27, 1830; *The Liberator* of February 19, 1831; J. B. McMaster, *A History of the People of the United States*, New York, 1906, Vol. VI, p. 71.

65. *Niles' Weekly Register, Ibid.*, 87; S. E. Morison, *The Life and Letters of Harrison Gray Otis, Federalist 1765-1848*, Boston and New York, Vol. II, p. 257.

66. *Acts passed at a General Assembly . . . . of Virginia . . . . one thousand eight hundred and thirty . . . . ,* Richmond, 1831, pp. 107-108. (An act passed April 13 1831, forbade trading with slaves without owner's permission—*Ibid.*, p. 130.) The former is given almost in full in *Slavery Agitation in Virginia 1829-1832*—Baltimore, 1930, *op. cit.*, pp. 52-53; *The American Annual Register*, 1830-1831, Boston, N.Y., 1832, p. 347; *Life, Travels and Opinions of Benjamin Lundy . . . . op. cit.*, Phila., 1847, p. 237.

NAT TURNER'S SLAVE REBELLION

It appears that the Walker pamphlet was the immediate cause, too, for the passage of laws[67] in Georgia, Louisiana, North Carolina, and Mississippi. The law passed by the Georgia legislature of 1829 provided for a forty day quarantine on all vessels carrying free Negroes; ". . . . renders capital the circulation of pamphlets of evil tendency among our domestics; makes penal the teaching of free persons of color or slaves to read or write; and prohibits the introduction of slaves into this state for sale."[68] According, however, to Garrison,[69] the last feature of this law ". . . . is almost a dead letter." There is an interesting item in Niles[70] which indicates the practical difficulties involved in attempting to keep a people illiterate: "The grand jury of Richmond County, Georgia, have presented it as a nuisance or crime, that printers and publishers throughout the state, but particularly in the City of Augusta, employ negroes in the different departments of their establishments; thereby affording a source of information to that class of our population which sound policy forbids." Nothing appears to have been done about this, though some regulations adopted soon after the Turner Revolt may have affected the employment of Negroes in printing establishments, as elsewhere.

There were several laws pertinent to this work passed by the two legislatures of North Carolina preceding the Turner Revolt. At the session of 1828-1829[71] it was declared illegal to sell, barter, or exchange any "fire arms, powder, or shot, or lead" to, or with, any slave not commissioned to purchase such merchandise by his owner. The white here

---

67. These laws are, at times, referred to as though they came after the Turner Revolt—See G. H. Barnes, *The Anti-Slavery Impulse 1830-1844*, New York & London, 1933, p. 51; *American History for Colleges*, D. S. Muzzey, J. A. Krout, Boston, 1933, p. 253.
68. *Niles' Weekly Register*, XXXVII, 341, Jan. 16, 1830; the section on teaching is in G. M. Stroud, *A Sketch of the laws relating to slavery* . . . . second edition, Phila., 1856, p. 141.
69. The *Liberator*, Jan. 8, 1831, Vol. I, p. 7.
70. *Niles' Weekly Register*, XXXVII, 275, Dec. 26, 1829.
71. *Acts of the General Assembly of the State of North Carolina*, at the session of 1828-1829, Raleigh, 1829, p. 19. (In effect May 1, 1830.)

28

was to be fined $100 and imprisoned for three months, a free Negro was to be lashed 39 times. In the session of 1830-1831 several laws applying to Negroes were passed. One forbade the marriage of free Negroes and whites and also prohibited a free Negro from marrying or cohabiting with a slave. Another law provided that anyone who, in any way, aided in the circulation or preparation of any writing tending ".... to excite insurrection, conspiracy or resistance in the slaves or free negroes" was, for the first offense, to be pilloried, whipped and imprisoned for one year. For the second offense the penalty was death without benefit of clergy. He who attempted to do the same by words was to receive 39 lashes and a year's imprisonment, with death, again, for the second offense. It was also made illegal to teach a slave to read or write, "figures exempted," nor was any slave to be given any book or pamphlet. A white who disobeyed was to be fined not less than $100 and not more than $200. If the guilty one was a free Negro he might be fined or imprisoned or whipped (from 20 to 39 lashes) at the discretion of the court. Anyone aiding a runaway slave was subject to a $100 fine. Provision was also made for the calling out and paying the militia to stop depredations of runaway slaves (which, as previously stated, were considerable in 1830) in seven counties. There were also four regulations concerning only free Negroes. One restricted their peddling to their own county, and a license for this was required. An emancipated Negro had to leave the state within 90 days, and if any free Negro remained out of the State for over 90 days he was not allowed to return, unless sickness had delayed him. A quarantine of 30 days on all ships having free Negroes was established.

This long list of laws was not sufficient to allay the fears of these legislators and it was further provided that in the counties of Brunswick and New Hanover each plantation having 15 slaves or more over twelve years of age was to have at least one white person on it. In fifteen counties, including the two just mentioned, no slave unaccompanied by his master or his written permission was to attend muster or election grounds.[72]

In Louisiana, on April 1, 1829, a law[73] went into effect to regulate more thoroughly the purchasing of slaves from other states. It was required that for each slave over twelve years old, the purchaser was to have a certificate signed by at least two freeholders of the county in which the sale was made giving a full description of the slave and stating that he had been guilty of no plotting or other criminal offense and had not resided in a county, state or territory during an insurrection or conspiracy. Governor A. B. Roman, in his message of November 14, 1831, when asking for new regulations, refers to this law and remarks about the "facility . . . . in deceiving." A defect, remedied after the Turner Revolt, was that no appropriation to enforce this law was made. Several months later two new regulations[74] were passed. One declared that free Negroes who had entered Louisiana since 1825 were to be expelled, the other attempted to restrict financial dealings with slaves. The state by an Act[75] passed in March, 1830, forbade the teaching of slaves to read or write under a penalty of imprisonment for ". . . . not less than one nor more than twelve months."

In the State of Mississippi the more severe slave laws started on January 28, 1829, when a law[76] was passed declar-

---

72. *Acts passed by the General Assembly of the State of North Carolina* at the session of 1830-1831, Raleigh, 1831, pp. 9, 10, 11, 12, 16, 29, 119, 128, 129, 130.; G. M. Stroud, *A Sketch of the laws relating to slavery*, op. cit., gives the regulations on teaching, pp. 141-142; *Life, Travels and Opinions of Benjamin Lundy*, op. cit., mentions, in general terms, some of the laws, p. 256 n.; some are mentioned in a similar way in H. M. Wagstaff, *State Rights and Political Parties in North Carolina*, J. Hopkins Un. Studies, XVII, No. 7-8, Baltimore, 1899, p. 100-1.

73. *Acts passed at the first session of the ninth legislature of . . . . Louisiana . . . .* New Orleans, 1829, pp. 38 ff. For Governor's message see The *Atlas*, New York, Vol. IV, p. 103, Dec. 10, 1831.

74. *Niles' Weekly Register*, (Baltimore) XXXVIII, p. 157, Apr. 24, 1830.

75. G. M. Stroud, *A Sketch . . . . op. cit.*, p. 142 (Second edition.)

76. *A digest of the laws of Mississippi . . . . including the acts of the session of 1839.* T. J. F. Alden, J. A. Van Hoesen, New York, 1839, p. 767.

ing that any slave who committed ".... an assault and bat-
tery ...." with intent to kill, on a white, ".... where implied
malice only is shewn ...." was to be lashed 100 times for
each of three successive days. The assembly of this state in
1830[77] passed a law forbidding all to ".... print, write, circu-
late or put forth ...., ," or cause any of these to be done,
".... any book, paper, magazine, pamphlet, handbill, or
circular in this state, containing any sentiment, doctrine, advice or innuendos calculated to produce a disorderly, dangerous or rebellious disaffection among the colored population."
A white who disobeyed this was to be fined from $100 to
$1,000 and imprisoned from three to twelve months. A guilty
Negro was to suffer death. Other regulations in this act
forbade the employment of Negroes ".... in the setting of
types." No free Negro was to keep a house of entertainment
or ".... to vend any goods, wares, merchandise or spirituous
liquors ...." under a penalty of from 20 to 50 lashes.

There was, finally, in the closing months of 1829, a strong
effort made to have a constitutional convention meet in
Kentucky, which, it seems, was defeated by one vote. One of
the objects of this constitutional convention was to have
been the abolition of slavery.[78] In 1830 a bill to abolish slavery was, in the House,[79] postponed indefinitely by a vote of
18 to 11. The agitation over the question of a constitutional
convention in Kentucky moved Niles to make this remark:[80]
"We have no desire to meddle with the general question of
slavery—it *must* be met sometime, though probably not in
our day." Soon, very soon, this idea of postponement, neutrality, indifference, was to disappear and the generation of
crisis was to appear.

One may, then, observe in the half-decade preceding the

---

77. *Laws of the State of Mississippi passed at the 14th session of the
    General Assembly* .... Jackson, 1830, pp. 86-88.
78. *Niles' Weekly Register*, XXXVII, p. 357, January 16, 1830.
79. *Life, Travels and Opinions of Benjamin Lundy* .... compiled under
    the direction and on behalf of his children, Phila., 1847, p. 237.
80. *Niles' Weekly Register*, op. cit., p. 357. (emphasis in original).

Turner Revolt, economic depression throughout the South and within the locale of the Revolt. One may observe maldistribution of population, and grumblings and rumblings emanating from the enslaved portion of the population throughout the Western hemisphere. One may observe the beginnings of a change in anti-slavery agitation, here and abroad, and uneasiness due to Cuba and Texas. He notes petitions, publications, letters, bills, laws, indicating uncertainty, fear, perplexity.

And then, beneath this boiling pot, came a sudden added blast of fire, the creator of which was named Nat, formerly the slave of one Benjamin Turner.

THE EVENT

It may at once be said that there are features of the Turner Revolt that are still uncertain and probably will remain so. Any statement purporting to give the precise number of Negroes who took part in the Revolt, or the exact number of victims, white or Negro, is to be suspiciously regarded. What appear to be fairly good approximations may be made.

It is thought, however, to be possible with the available evidence, to answer other and more important questions. The causes and the purposes of the event may be discerned. Whether what is today to be seen in this connection is all that really existed over one hundred years ago, cannot be said, but causes and purposes are yet visible and appear to be sufficient to explain the Revolt. Similarly, there are many results that appear, some more clearly than others, which will be discussed later.

Concerning the Turner Revolt there is unanimity on two things, and only on two things. First, all agree it took place, or, at least, started (whether it was local or not will be dealt with later) in Southampton County and, second, that the leader was Nat Turner. The former has been sufficiently described, but what sort of person was Nat?

A: NAT TURNER, THE MAN

The year eighteen hundred was a fateful one for American slavery. It was then that John Brown was born, that Gabriel's revolt occurred and that Vesey purchased the ownership of his own body, and it was then, too, on October

33

2, that Nat Turner was born.[1] He was, then, almost 31 years old at the time of the Revolt. The following description of him was given,[2] together with the announcement of a reward of $500 for his capture, by the Governor of Virginia, John Floyd: "Nat is between 30 and 35 years old, 5 feet 6 or 8 inches high, weighs between 150 and 160 pounds, rather bright complexion, but not a mulatto, broad shoulders, large flat nose, large eyes, broad flat feet, rather knock-kneed, walks brisk and active, hair on top of the head very thin, no beard, except on the upper lip and the top of the chin, a scar on one of his temples, also one on the back of his neck, a large knot on one of his bones of right arm, near the wrist, produced by a blow."

Very naturally, William Lloyd Garrison in commenting upon this description, pointed[3] to these scars as explaining Turner's actions. But the Richmond *Enquirer*[4] assured its readers that Turner got two of his bruises in fights with Negroes and one of them, that on his temple, through a mule's kick. Of course Drewry[5] accepts the explanation of the southern newspaper and also points out, correctly, that Turner stated his last master, Joseph Travis, had been kindly.[6] But Nat had had other masters like Benjamin Turner and Putnam Moore, and he had[7] (though Mr. Drewry[8] omits mention of this) run away from one of these (which

---

1. *The Confessions,* op. cit., Thomas Gray, Baltimore, 1831, p. 4. Only coincidence is meant to be shown here, not "prenatal influence" which J. W. Cromwell sees—*Journal of Negro History,* Vol. 5, (1920) No. 2, April, "The Aftermath of Nat Turner's Insurrection", p. 208.
   The information on Vesey is in *An Account of some of the principal slave insurrections,* and others, which have occurred, or been attempted, in the United States . . . New York, 1860, by Joshua Coffin, p. 33.
2. The *National Intelligencer,* Washington, Sept. 24, 1831.
3. The *Liberator,* October 1, 1831, Vol. I, p. 159.
4. Richmond *Enquirer,* October 25, 1831.
5. W. S. Drewry, *The Southampton Insurrection,* Washington, 1900, p. 173. Note 1.
6. *The Confessions* . . . . p. 11.
7. *The Confessions* . . . . p. 9.
8. In fact Drewry says that "Nat himself, up to the time of the insurrection had been faithful and highly trusted"; p. 28 of *The Southampton Insurrection,* op. cit.

is not certain[9]) after a change in overseers. Moreover, Drewry's[10] own description of Nat does not aptly characterize one who is given to fighting. "From childhood Nat was very religious, truthful and honest, 'never owning a dollar, never uttering an oath, never drinking intoxicating liquors, and never committing a theft.'"

As a matter of fact, whether Turner's scars were caused by the kick of a mule or the whip of a white man, or both, it seems fairly clear that his motivation was not personal vengeance. The question of motivation, both of Nat and of his followers, will shortly be discussed in detail. Here suffice it to say that the conclusion of that examination will be that Nat Turner sought the liberation of the Negro people.

But, to return to the personality of Turner: An examination of the evidence reveals a highly intelligent man who finds it impossible to accept the status quo and discovers his rationalization for his rebellious feelings in religion. James C. Ballagh's[11] descriptive phrase "well-educated" is not well chosen for it implies formal instruction. Nat himself[12] was unable to account for his ability to read and write, though this is often ascribed to his parents' instructions. But it is certain that he was literate and that he read and reread the Bible. He also appears to have been gifted mechanically. It is possible that he owed part of his revolutionary spirit to

9. B. B. Weeks, *Magazine of American History*, XXV, June, 1891, op. cit., p. 450 says that Turner repaid Joseph Travis' kindness by running away. Turner makes it clear that he ran away in 1825 and became the slave of Travis in 1830. From whom he ran away is not certain, but he certainly did not run away from Joseph Travis. *Confessions*, p. 9, 11.

10. *The Southampton Insurrection*, Washington, 1900, by W. S. Drewry, p. 28. He does not say whom he is quoting. Similar, though not precisely the same words are used by Thomas Gray in the *Confessions*, p. 18.

11. J. C. Ballagh, *A History of Slavery in Virginia*, Johns Hopkins Un. Studies . . . . Extra Volume XXIV, Baltimore, 1902, p. 93.

12. The rest of this paragraph is taken from *The Confessions* passim. The quotations are on pp. 7, 8, 9. The first quotation is given by W. S. Drewry, *The Southampton Insurrection*, op. cit., 29.

35

his father, who, when Nat was a boy, ran away and was never recovered. But the supreme influence in his life undoubtedly was religion, as he understood it. Nat, himself, thought this was largely due to the many religious people who surrounded him in his youth, particularly, he says, his grandmother. These people noticed his ". . . . uncommon intelligence for a child, remarked I had too much sense to be raised, and if I was I would never be of any service to any one as a slave." Since there is no disagreement on this point one more quotation will suffice. "As I was praying one day at my plough, the spirit spoke to me, saying, 'Seek ye the kingdom of Heaven and all things shall be added unto you.' *Question* (by Thomas Gray)—What do you mean by the Spirit? *Answer*: The spirit that spoke to the prophets in former days—and I was greatly astonished, and for two years prayed continually, whenever my duty would permit—and then again I had the same revelation, which fully confirmed me in the impression that I was ordained for some great purpose in the hands of the Almighty."

Drewry states[13] that Turner was an "overseer" and U. B. Phillips describes him as a "foreman." Neither one nor the other tells where he got his information. Perhaps Drewry heard this from one of the people he interviewed as to their recollections of Nat going back some seventy years—not very good evidence. Phillips' choice of a word is better, for while a slave might be a foreman, he was never an overseer. But where his information was obtained is unknown. Nothing has been seen to substantiate either Drewry or Phillips.

Phillips' terminology is in another respect an improvement over Drewry's and here appears to be well-founded. Drewry thinks that Turner was a "Baptist preacher," but Phillips states that he was a "Baptist exhorter."[14] While it is a fair assumption that Turner did not adhere to a com-

---

13. W. S. Drewry, *Ibid.*, p. 27; U. B. Phillips, *American Negro Slavery* . . . . New York, London, 1918, p. 480.
14. W. S. Drewry, *Ibid.*, pp. 26, 27; U. B. Phillips, Ibid., p. 480.

plete theological system, he did practice one distinctive feature of the Baptist faith, i.e., baptism by immersion, as he
himself states[15] in discussing the case of a white man,
Ethelred T. Brantley, whom Turner prevailed upon to cease
"from his wickedness."

Some[16] have said with Drewry that he was a preacher,
others,[17] fewer, have denied this. It is clear that Turner was
not a regularly ordained minister, or, indeed, a properly
enrolled member, of any church,[18] but that, being admired
and respected by his fellow slaves,[19] he often spoke to them
on the Sabbath get-togethers. The word "exhorter" accurately describes Nat Turner. It is important that the contemporary accounts of the revolt referred to him, generally, as
a preacher; this helps explain certain laws enacted after the
Revolt. One evidence of this contemporary opinion will be
quoted. This piece of evidence[20] is selected because, so far
as is known, the source has never been used, and because
it is of excellent quality. Clearly the writer did not expect
posterity to read it and it was written less than one week
after the event. The letter is addressed to Thomas Ruffin,
then Judge of the Supreme Court of North Carolina. It was
written by one E. P. Guion and dated, "Raleigh, Sunday
August 28th, 1831." The part pertinent here runs as follows:
"It is strange to me that men can be so blind and Infatuate
as to be advocates of Negroes Preaching to negroes no dout
that these veery Slaves would have Remained quiet but for

15. *The Confessions* . . . . Thomas Gray, Baltimore, 1831, p. 11.
16. For examples see *The Atlas*, New York, Sept. 10, 1831, quoting the
Richmond *Compiler* of Aug. 29; J. C. Ballagh, *A History of Slavery
in Virginia, op. cit.*, p. 93; *American Annual Register*, 1830-1831,
Boston and New York, 1832, p. 349.
17. As examples see, The *National Intelligencer*, Washington, Sept. 10,
1831; J. W. Cromwell, *Journal of Negro History*, Vol. 5, *op. cit.*,
209; Benjamin Brawley, *A Social History of the American Negro*
. . . . New York, 1921, p. 141.
18. *New York Evening Post*, October 10, 1831.
19. *The Confessions* . . . . pp. 8-9.
20. *The Papers of Thomas Ruffin* collected and edited by J. G. de Roulhac
Hamilton, Raleigh, North Carolina, 1918, (publication of the N. C.
Historical Commission), Vol. II, p. 45.

this fanatic Black that has excited them in this diabolical deed some of them were wounded and in the aggonies of Death declared that they was going happy fore that God had a hand in what they had been doing they also had a story among them that the English was to assist them."

B: CAUSE AND MOTIVE

What were the causation and the motivation of the Turner Revolt? The former, which, it is felt, is more deep-seated, more prolonged, more objective than the latter, has been displayed in some detail in the preceding pages. This cannot be *proven*, as can a result in chemistry, but it seems correct to say that the Turner Revolt was not merely a remarkable coincidence agreeing with the temper of the half-decade preceding it. Rather, just as the laws, petitions, plots, revolts, intrigues of that period were manifestations of the times, of economic depression, of sociological maladjustment, of uncertainty, of fast and vast changes, and in turn helped create the spirit of those times, so the Turner Revolt appears to be a manifestation of this spirit, and a direct and indirect influence itself in developing the spirit and accounting for the events in the time immediately following its occurrence.

The evidence concerning the motivation of Nat Turner and of those who fought with him is fairly definite. Yet contemporary and later writers have offered varied hypothesis as to the motivation. These take three forms. It is said (1) that the motive is unknown, (2) that plunder was the object, (3) that liberty was sought; some here saying only because of the incitations of the abolitionists, others maintaining that the desire for liberty needed and had no such extraneous creator but sprang from the brains and the hearts of the Negroes themselves.

The early newspaper accounts[21] at times stated that

---

21. Richmond *Enquirer*, August 30, 1831; editor of the Richmond Whig, quoted by the *Atlas*, New York, Vol. 4, p. 7, September 17, 1831.

"Their ultimate object . . . . (is) not yet explained." But in a work written[22] over fifty years after the event one is again informed that Turner's ". . . . motives remain unknown."

The second explanation was widely adopted by contemporaries. The papers[23] of the time kept referring to the Negroes as "banditti" and to Nat Turner as the "bandit" and Governor Floyd, in his message to the Virginia Legislature of 1831-32, refers to "a banditti of slaves."[24] A North Carolina paper printed a letter telling of the discovery of a plot led by a Negro called Fed. Said the writer:[25] "Fed's plan, I have no doubt, was like that of Nat in Virginia, to obtain whatever money he could from the negroes, and more by plunder, then make his escape, and leave his poor deluded followers to shift for themselves." Niles also, at first, reported[26] that ". . . . it is believed to have originated only in a design to plunder and not with a view to a more important object. . . . ." Writing some weeks later Amos Gilbert observes[27] the confusion in the Southern papers on this point. "It appears from the southern papers that an insurrection recently took place with some colored people of Southampton County Va.; or rather perhaps that some fugitive slaves had killed a number of persons in their pursuit of plunder."

But the majority of the less immediate contemporary accounts and almost all of the later commentators agree that "a more important object," liberty, did exist. Some state this implicitly when they excoriate the abolitionists for having, as they affirm, brought on the revolt; others, observing no

---

22. J. E. Cooke, *Virginia, A History of the People,* (American Commonwealths, editor, H. E. Scudder), Boston, 1883, p. 486.
23. As examples, Richmond *Enquirer,* August 30, October 18, November 8, 1831.
24. *Journal of the House of Delegates of the Commonwealth of Virginia* . . . . 1831, Richmond, no pagination; the message is also in *Niles' Weekly Register,* XLI, 350, Jan 7, 1832.
25. Richmond *Enquirer,* November 26, 1831, quoting Raleigh Register (n.d.)
26. *Niles' Weekly Register,* XL, 455, August 27, 1831.
27. Article signed "A.G" in the *Free Enquirer,* New York, Vol. III, No. 47, September 17, 1831.

proof of that, often add a saving statement about the possibility of Turner's having read or met the abolitionists.

Governor John Floyd in his message of December 6, 1831, already referred to,[28] states that Negro preachers and northern abolitionists were responsible for the Revolt. Mrs. Lawrence Lewis,[29] a niece of George Washington, in a letter dated, Alexandria, October 17, 1831, writes to her friend, the Mayor of Boston, Harrison Gray Otis that ". . . . to the Editor of the 'Liberator' . . . . we owe in *greatest measure* this calamity." W. Gilmore Simms,[30] in his review of Harriet Martineau's book on the United States, objects to her statement, which he quotes in part, and not quite accurately, to the effect that the Revolt happened before the "abolition movement began." "Our author," says Mr. Simms, "confounds cause with effect. She should have said that the Southampton insurrection broke out before the secret workings of the abolitionists had been generally detected or suspected."

A. B. Hart[31] declares that the Walker pamphlet ". . . . may possibly have influenced the Nat Turner insurrection of 1831. . . . ." This very guarded statement is cited by H. A. Herbert to substantiate his[32] idea that northern agitators were responsible for the Revolt. It is very possible that Professor Hart made his statement on the basis of the opinion of Benjamin Lundy[33] who believed that Nat Turner ". . . . had prob-

---

28. ante, note 24, *Niles' Weekly Register*, XLI, 350, Jan. 7, 1832.
29. S. E. Morison, *The Life and letters of Harrison Gray Otis* . . . . Boston and New York, 1913, Vol. II, p. 260. (emphasis in original).
30. "The Morals of Slavery . . . ." in *The Pro-Slavery Argument* . . . . Chancellor Harper, Governor Hammond, Dr. Simms, and Professor Dew, Charleston, 1852, p. 223. Miss Martineau's statement is in her *Society in America*, New York and London, 1837, Fourth edition, Vol. I, p. 378.
31. A. B. Hart, *Slavery and Abolition 1831-1841* (Vol. 16 of the *American Nation* series, edited by A. B. Hart), N.Y. & London, 1906, pp. 217-218.
32. Hilary A. Herbert, *The Abolition Crusade and its consequences* . . . . New York, 1912, p. 60.
33. *Life, Travels and Opinions of Benjamin Lundy* . . . . op. cit., Philadelphia, 1847, p. 249, 247, also p. 237.

ably seen . . . ." the pamphlet and thought it ". . . . probable
. . . . that the conspiracies (the Turner conspiracy and those
that followed) were instigated chiefly by the before mentioned pamphlet of David Walker, if in fact they owed their
origin to any publication whatever." R. A. Brock[34] is also of
the opinion that abolitionist propaganda directly influenced
Nat Turner. This gentleman is cited by W. S. Drewry[35] who
agrees with him. Carter G. Woodson also at least implies
that abolitionist literature was important in bringing on the
Revolt.[36]

Others, fewer, deny that there is discernible any connection between this propaganda and the outbreak of the
Revolt. First in this group is, of course, William Lloyd Garrison himself,[37] who persistently and truthfully denied ad-
vising the Negroes to use force and declared: "We have not
a single white or black subscriber south of the Potomac." As
James Ford Rhodes states:[38] "The assertion that slavery is a
damning crime is one thing; the actual incitement of slaves
to insurrection is another." Yet, while S. E. Morison[39] recog-
nizes that ". . . . Garrison always disclaimed any intent of
inciting slave insurrection" he thinks that the Turner Revolt
was described by him ". . . . in so truculent a manner as fairly to justify the Southern suspicions of his motives." The
word "truculent" is not too strong. In the *Liberator*[40] first
giving an account of the Revolt is this paragraph: "Ye patri-

---

34. "Miscellaneous Papers 1672-1865" in *Collections of the Virginia History Society,* new series, VI, Richmond, 1887 p. 24 not 69.
35. *The Southampton Insurrection, op. cit.,* p. 150.
36. *The Education of the Negro prior to 1861* . . . ., New York and London, 1915, p. 163.
37. The *Liberator,* Sept. 24, 1831, Vol. I, p. 155.
38. *History of the United States from the compromise of 1850,* New York, 1896, Vol. I, p. 57.
39. *Life and Letters of Harrison Gray Otis* . . . . Boston and N.Y., 1913, Vol. II, p. 261.
40. The *Liberator* (Boston), Vol. I, p. 143, Sept. 3, 1831; quoted, in part, in *William Lloyd Garrison 1805-1879* . . . ., by his children, W. P. and F. J. Garrison, New York, 1885. Vol. I, p. 250.

otic hyprocites! ye panegyrists of Frenchmen, Greeks, and Poles! ye Christian declaimers for liberty! ye valiant sticklers for equal rights among yourselves! ye haters of aristocracy! ye assailants of monarchy! ye republican nullifiers! ye treasonable disunionists! be dumb! Cast no reproach upon the conduct of the slaves, but let your lips and cheeks wear the blisters of condemnation." Certainly this is truculent, but not merely because of its exclamation marks. Nothing is more fierce, more uncompromising than truth.

The fact is that never has an iota of evidence been submitted to show that any abolitionist propaganda, of the Walker, Garrison, or milder type, had any connection whatsoever with bringing on the Turner Revolt.[41] Certainly one may say with A. B. Hart that it is "possible" the Walker pamphlet influenced Turner. It is also possible that some study of Napoleon influenced Turner and he decided that ". . . . I was ordained for some great purpose in the hands of the Almighty."[42] There is as much proof for the one possibility as for the other. So when Burgess[43] states that "we shall probably never know whether there was [a connection between the propaganda and the event] or not," everything depends on what is meant by "know." The statement that there was no such connection is at least as justified as much of historical knowledge.

The previous writers, who asserted the abolitionists were responsible for the event, imply thereby that liberty was sought. And the origin of this seeking may clearly be seen in the mind of Nat Turner. It dawned and arose and filled his consciousness without having received any direct, definite extraneous stimulation. Thomas Gray's so-called *Con-*

---

41. J. Macy, *The Anti-Slavery Crusade* . . . . (*Chronicles of America* V. 28, edited by A. Johnson), New Haven, Toronto, London, 1921, p. 59 says this concerning Garrison; see also G. H. Barnes, *The Anti-Slavery Impulse 1830-1844* . . . . N.Y. & London, 1933, p. 51.
42. *The Confessions*, p. 9.
43. J. W. Burgess, *The Middle Period 1817-1858*, New York, 1918, p. 249.

fessions tells the story. Here one learns that Nat Turner was able to read and that he read and lived through within himself the stories of the Bible. He was intelligent and well enough treated to want to be better treated.[44]

Certainly, Nat ran away and stayed away for thirty days. But then he returned for ". . . . the Spirit appeared to me and said I had my wishes directed to the things of this world, and not to the kingdom of Heaven, and that I should return to the service of my earthly master. . . . ." But the other Negroes, the rank and file, as it might today be put ". . . . found fault, and murmured (sic) against me, saying that if they had my sense they would not serve any master in the world."[45]

Turner stated,[46] further, that ". . . . on the 12th of May, 1828, I heard a loud noise in the heavens, and the Spirit instantly appeared to me and said the Serpent was loosened, and Christ had laid down the yoke he had borne for the sins of men, and that I should take it on and fight against the Serpent, for the time was fast approaching when the first should be last and the last should be first. *Question*: (by T. Gray) Do you not find yourself mistaken now? *Answer*: Was not Christ crucified. . . . ." This last answer does not agree very well with the letter[47] from Mr. T. Trezvant to the editors of the Norfolk *Beacon*, of October 31: "He (Nat Turner) acknowledges himself a coward . . . . he acknowledges now that the revelation was misinterpreted by him . . . . he is now convinced that he has done wrong, and advises all other Negroes not to follow his example." It is possible that the mob

---

44. Frederick Douglass' speech at Moorfields, England, May 12, 1846— ". . . . the better you treat a slave, the more you destroy his value as a slave . . . . as soon as the blow was not to be feared, then came the longing for liberty." C. G. Woodson, *Negro Orators and their Orations*, Washington, 1925, p. 162.
45. *The Confessions*, pp. 9, 10. Thomas Gray, Baltimore, 1831.
46. *Ibid.*, p. 11, quoted, not accurately, by W. S. Drewry, *The Southampton Insurrections*, Washington, 1900, p. 33.
47. In the Richmond *Enquirer* of November 8, 1831.

which, it is said,[48] pricked, punched, and barrel-rolled Turner after he was caught, sought words like that from him, but the words of Nat Turner already given, and those to follow, refute this propaganda from Mr. Trezvant, the purpose of which is given in his last sentence.

Turner waited for a sign from his God. This came to him in the form of a solar eclipse of February 1831. Nat then told four companions that it was time to prepare for the revolt. And what day was selected?—July 4th. This moved William H. Parker to exclaim:[49] "This national holiday, hallowed as a day of liberty and peace (!) consecrated to the memories of the brave, patriotic heroes of the Revolution, was to be set apart for the complete destruction of the lives of their sons, and their property by a band of ferocious miscreants. Shame, shame! to thus pervert that sacred day and stain it with gory deeds!" How complexion affects reason!

But Nat Turner was ill on July 4th. Very naturally, then, it was necessary to wait for another sign. And, again, the peculiar appearance of the sun, this time on Saturday, the 13th of August, when it had a "greenish blue color," seems to have been accepted as the sign. According to Drewry, Nat Turner exhorted at a meeting of Negroes in the southern part of Southampton not in North Carolina, (as has been said)[51] where some of the Negroes ". . . signified their willingness to co-operate with him by wearing around their

---

48. W. S. Drewry, *The Southampton Insurrection*, pp. 145-150; given also in J. E. Cutler, *Lynch Law*, an investigation into the history of lynching in the United States, New York, London, Bombay, 1905, p. 93. This is contradicted by account in the *Atlas*, Vol. 4, p. 71, Nov. 12, 1831, quoting the Petersburg *Intelligencer* (n.d.) ". . . . not the least personal violence was offered to Nat . . . ." The eclipse is noted in *The Confessions*, p. 11.

49. "The Nat Turner Insurrection", W. H. Parker, in *Old Virginia Yarns*, V. 1, no. 1, Jan. 1893, p. 18. (no title page—the above is written in pencil—copy in the Virginia State Library, Richmond).

50. *New York Evening Post*, August 26, 1831; S. B. Weeks, *Magazine of American History*, XXV, June, 1891, p. 451.

51. "The 100th Anniversary of the Turner Revolt," by N. Stevens in *The Communist*, N.Y. August, 1931, Vol. X, No. 8, p. 739.

necks red bandanna handerchiefs . . ." The same author states that these Negroes also showed their "rebellious spirits" by trying "to ride over white people."[52] No reference is given and the ring of this is false. It is, however, certain that there was a meeting of conspirators in the afternoon of Sunday, August 21 and it was then decided, as was done, to start the revolt that evening.[53]

Nat was the last one to arrive at this meeting, purposely, as he stated. He seems to have appreciated the value of a dramatic entrance. He noticed a newcomer in the group: "I saluted them on coming up, and asked Will how came he there, he answered, his life was worth no more than others, and his liberty as dear to him. I asked him if he meant to obtain it? He said he would, or loose (sic) his life. This was enough to put him in full confidence." Such was the banditry of Nat Turner! And Turner, contrary to another of Mr. Trezvant's statements, did not believe he had "done wrong." As his lawyer stated, Turner pleaded not guilty ". . . saying to his counsel, that he did not feel so."[54]

There is what appears at first to be further evidence to substantiate the thesis that desire for liberty was Turner's motive. This is the speech which, according to G. W. Williams,[55] Turner made to his followers just before the Revolt started. The closing sentences reveal the gist of this: "Remember that ours is not war for robbery nor to satisfy our

52. *The Southampton Insurrection*, W. S. Drewry, *op. cit.*, p. 157.
53. *The Confessions*, p. 12. This date is followed by all writers, except three. The exceptions are—(Samuel Warner) *Authentic and impartial narrative of the tragical scene which was witnessed in Southampton County (Virginia) on Monday the 22d of August last* . . . . New York, 1831; J. B. McMaster (who used Warner pamphlet) *A History of the People* . . . . Vol. VI, p. 73 (night of August 22) New York, 1906; F. B. Sanborn, *Life and Letters of John Brown* . . . . Boston, 1891 (date as Aug. 23) p. 34, note 1.
54. *The Confessions*, p. 12 and 20. See also W. S. Drewry, *op. cit.*, p. 117
55. *History of the Negro race in America from 1619 to 1880* . . . . by George W. Williams, N. Y. 1883, Vol. II, 87-88; same speech quoted uncritically by H. P. Wilson, *John Brown soldier of fortune* . . . . Lawrence, Kansas, 1913, pp. 360-361.

passions; it is a *struggle for freedom*. Ours must be deeds, not words. Then let us away to the scene of action." This, it is believed, accurately describes Turner's feelings, but the entire speech flowed from Mr. Williams' oratorical powers, not Turner's.

It appears, then, that Nat Turner's main object was not plunder. But what about this followers? If one may judge by the conversation between Will and Turner previously quoted he may fairly say that among the original conspirators liberty loomed as the primary, perhaps as the sole, aim. And if Mr. Guion,[56] in his letter to Judge Thomas Ruffin, was accurate, it appears that this same desire animated some, at least, of the scores who later joined the Revolt.

But it is a fair assumption that not all who took part in this movement were solely or primarily motivated by the desire simply for freedom. If it were otherwise, the Nat Turner Revolt would be absolutely unique. It appears that money was taken,[57] but not even an approximation as to the amount is possible. It is also not certain whether the money was taken for itself or as a means to furthering the revolt. Drewry[58] is certain that ". . . each negro meditated returning home within a few days to take possession of his master's home." It would be interesting to know how Mr. Drewry knows what "each negro meditated" in 1831, but quite possibly this idea existed among some of them. Drewry, indeed, tells of one gentleman, Mr. Collin Kitchen, (and this depends upon the latter's memory going back seventy years) who found, after the suppression of the revolt, that his house and its possessions had been taken over by one of his slaves.

It has often been said[59] that a large number of the

---

56. Ante, *The Papers of Thomas Ruffin*, Vol. II, p. 45.
57. T. W. Higginson, "Nat Turner's Insurrection," *Atlantic Monthly*, Aug., 1861, Vol. 8, p. 176; W. S. Drewry, *The Southampton Insurrection*, Washington, 1900, p. 117.
58. W. S. Drewry, *op. cit.*, p. 117; p. 117 n. 2.
59. The *Atlas*, New York, September 10, 1831; *Encyclopaedia Britannica*, 14th edition, Vol. 22, p. 628; W. S. Drewry, *op. cit.*, p. 59.

Negroes who took part in the Revolt did so only under compulsion. As Higginson pointed[60] out, it was to be expected that, once the movement had been crushed, this would be offered as an extenuating circumstance. How many, then, if any, joined the Revolt only under duress cannot be said.

C: THE LIGHTNING STRIKES

No attempt will here be made to give a detailed picture of the proceedings of the Revolt. Accuracy is impossible, and the importance of it is very questionable. Moreover, the attempt has been made by Drewry[61] who devotes forty pages to it. This is really too detailed, for the reader is told[62] that one infant was temporarily spared because it "sweetly smiled" at the assailant. Violence is too horrible to need any such artistic touches, and that such embellishments are not of an historic nature needs no demonstration. This was a revolt and as Lincoln Steffens remarked to Eugene Debs, who was strongly deprecating the violence of the Bolshevik Revolution:[63] "True 'Gene. That's all true that you say. A revolution is no gentleman." Here Nat Turner, himself,[64] may be quoted: ". . . He (Nat Turner) says that indiscriminate massacre was not their intention after they obtained foothold, and was resorted to in the first instance to strike terror and alarm. Women and children would afterwards have been spared, and men too who ceased to resist."

Certain phases of the event will be examined. Attempts will be made to answer such questions as: How many

---

60. T. W. Higginson, *Atlantic Monthly*, Aug., 1861, *op. cit.*, 180-181.
61. W. S. Drewry, *op. cit.*, pp. 35-74.
62. *Ibid.*, p. 36.
63. *The Autobiography of Lincoln Steffens*, complete in one volume, New York, 1931, p. 844.
64. Richmond *Enquirer*, Nov. 8, 1831; T. W. Higginson gave this, without quotation marks, and as being stated by the editor of the *Enquirer*. The editor here was paraphrasing Turner. See *Atlantic Monthly*, V. 8, August, 1861, *op. cit.*, p. 176.

Negroes took part? How many people were killed *before* the Revolt was suppressed? Was there any connection between the poorer whites and the Negroes? How was the Revolt suppressed?

The first question may be answered only approximately —indeed, Nat Turner, himself, did not venture more. It appears that between sixty and eighty Negroes took part in the Revolt. But it is to be noticed that most of the contemporary figures were very much higher than this, thus making the extreme terror that ensued more understandable. The highest estimate[65] observed places the number at "six or eight hundred." Other contemporary accounts[66] put the number at from 150 to 300, but there is only one later writer, so far as is known, who gives the number as within that scope. J. B. McMaster[67] gives the number as two hundred.

There are, on the other hand, contemporary estimates, which fall within the range suggested as being probably accurate. From what Turner himself says[68] it is apparent that he thought his followers amounted to from 60 to 80. The Governor of Virginia[69] thought that there were no more than seventy slaves implicated at any time. The editor of the Richmond *Whig*, when he visited Southampton,[70] decided that ". . . the insurgents never exceeded 60 . . .". According to the Richmond *Compiler* of August 29th,[71] only about fifty Negroes took part. In the letter of E. P. Guion, already partly quoted, it is said:[72] ". . . it was thought that

---

65. *Niles' Weekly Register* (Baltimore) XL, Aug. 27, 1831, p. 456.
66. As examples, see *Ibid.*, XL, 455, 456; Richmond *Enquirer*, Aug. 26, 1831; (S. Warner) *Authentic and impartial narrative* . . . . *op. cit.*, New York, 1831, p. 10.
67. *A History of the people of the United States* . . . . N.Y. 1906, p. 73.
68. *The Confessions* . . . . , p. 14 ff.
69. *Niles' Weekly Register* (speech of Dec. 6, 1831), XLI, 350, January 7, 1832.
70. Richmond *Whig*, August 29, 1831.
71. Quoted in The *Atlas*, New York, Sept. 10, 1831.
72. Dated Raleigh, Aug. 28, 1831, in *The Papers of Thomas Ruffin*, edited by J. G. de Roulhae Hamilton, Raleigh, 1918, Vol. II, p. 46.

not more than sixty negroes at the most was (sic) in the Rebellion. . . ."

In comparing the two classes of evidence the second is clearly preferable and has been followed by all later writers,[73] with two exceptions. One has been mentioned. The other, who goes to the opposite extreme, is James C. Ballagh who states that ". . . the band grew . . . finally, to forty." Why that low number is selected is not explained. It appears, then, that probably from sixty to eighty Negroes fought with Nat Turner.

The number killed before the revolt was put down may, again, only be approximated, but more closely than the other. Whether any Negroes were then killed is not clear, but if any were the number was small. A contemporary report states that at one of the last encounters, that at the home of a Dr. Blount,[75] the Negroes left ". . . one killed (we believe) and one wounded . . ." Drewry states[76] that at the engagement which occurred at Parker's Field ". . . several of the Negroes . . ." were killed, but, as usual, no reference is given. Some,[77] on the other hand, have denied that any Negroes were killed while the actual revolt was in progress.

In the *Confessions* Thomas Gray gave the names of the whites killed. His list amounts to fifty-five. The same total is given in the pamphlet by Samuel Warner[78] and it is the

---

73. As examples, see: T. W. Higginson, *Atlantic Monthly, op. cit.,* Vol. 8, p. 176; W. D. Weatherford and C. S. Johnson, *Race Relations,* N.Y., 1934, p. 271: Drewry, *op. cit.,* p. 96, (this is, however, contradicted by a statement on p. 86); U. B. Phillips, *American Negro Slavery* . . . . New York, London, 1918, p. 481.
74. *A History of Slavery in Virginia, op. cit.,* Baltimore, 1902, p. 93.
75. Quoting the editor of the Richmond *Whig* in the *Atlas,* Vol. 4, p. 7, September 17, 1831.
76. *The Southampton Insurrection,* Washington, 1900, p. 65.
77. See: T. W. Higginson, *Atlantic Monthly, op. cit.,* p. 176; J. W. Cromwell, "The Aftermath of Nat Turner's Insurrection", *Journal of Negro History* (1920, Vol V, p. 214.)
78. In *Confessions,* p 22;. (S. Warner) *Authentic and impartial narrative* . . . . N.Y., 1831, the total is in the title—see bibliography.

figure given by a number of later writers.[79] Drewry[80] reprints the list given by Gray and states that one overseer is omitted. No list gives the name of Shepherd Lee, 24 years old, who, in a genealogy of the Lee family[81] of York County, Virginia, is mentioned as ". . . killed in 1831 in Nat Turner's Insurrection. . . ." This brings the number killed to fifty-seven. Very often, however,[82] a figure in the sixties is given. Only three figures higher than this have been seen.[83] Miss Martineau states that ". . . . upwards of seventy white, chiefly women and children . . . ." were killed. This figure, as she states, was gotten from hearsay. James K. Paulding asked a planter of eastern Virginia to describe conditions. This planter refers to Turner, and there is a footnote, apparently by Paulding, as follows: "The leader of the insurrection in Lower Virginia, in which upwards of a hundred white persons, principally women and children, were massacred in cold blood." The highest estimate, two hundred killed, appeared in one of the earliest contemporary guesses. It appears that more than fifty-five but less than sixty-five whites were killed in Southampton County within the approximately 40 hours that the Revolt raged.

79. As examples see: *Harper's Encyclopaedia of United States History* . . . . N.Y., London, 1902, Vol. IX, p. 133; U. B. Phillips, *American Negro Slavery* . . . . N.Y. & London, 1918, 481; *Race Relations* by W. D. Weatherford, C. S. Johnson, *op. cit.*, p. 271, N.Y. 1934.
80. W. S. Drewry, *op. cit.*, p. 196.
81. *William and Mary College Quarterly Historical Magazine*, Vol. XXIV, (first series) 1915, Richmond, p. 52.
82. J. W. Cromwell, *op. cit.*, *Journal of Negro History*, V. 214; *Anti-Slavery Manual* . . . . by Rev. LeRoy Sunderland, second edition, 1837, N.Y., p. 87; The *Atlas*, *op. cit.*, Vol. 4, p. 6, Sept. 17, 1831; J. C. Ballagh, *History of Slavery in Virginia*, *op. cit.*, p. 93; G. M. Weston, *The Progress of Slavery in the United States*, Washington, 1857, p. 192; J. W. Burgess, *The Middle Period 1817-1858*, N.Y. 1898, p. 249; L. P. Stryker, *Andrew Johnson, a study in courage*, N.Y., 1929, p. 45—and others—
83. *Society in America, fourth edition*, New York, London, 1837, Vol. I, 378; J. K. Paulding, *Slavery in the United States*, N.Y. 1836, p. 192, also p. 56—the planter was George E. Harrison—*Virginia Magazine of History and Biography*, Richmond, XXVI, 1928, p. 277 n; *N.Y. Evening Post*, Aug. 26, 1831.

D: WERE THERE WHITE ALLIES?

Some of the first contemporary accounts[84] stated that the Revolt was led by a few whites, in no case more than three. Governor Floyd[85] in his message of December 6, 1831 hinted that the rebellious spirit was "not confined to the slaves." The close friendship between Nat and a white man, E. T. Brantley, has been mentioned. T. W. Higginson tells[86] what appears to be a story he invented of Nat Turner, at a meeting of Negro conspirators, sending some eavesdropping poor whites back to their homes with words of good advice, who then ". . . . were better friends than ever to Prophet Nat." Drewry states[87] that Turner ". . . . is said to have passed the home of some poor white people because he considered it useless to kill those who thought no better of themselves than they did of negroes." The tradition of Turner's behavior here may be accurate.

Better evidence has been unearthed by Mr. James H. Johnston.[88] This is a letter forming part of Governor Floyd's collected papers on "Slaves and Free Negroes." Although the letter is of considerable length it will be given in full for it is of great interest. The letter is addressed to:

'Ben Lee in great haste
mail speadily
Richmond swift.'
Chesterfield County
August 29, 1831.

My old fellow
Ben—
You will tell or acquaint every servant in Richmond and

---

84. Richmond *Enquirer*, Aug. 26, 1831; *Niles' Weekly Register*, XL, 456, Aug. 27, 1831; *Ibid*, XLI, p. 4, September 3, 1831.
85. *Journal of the House of Delegates* . . . .1831-1832, no pagination; this may be found in H. Wilson, *History of the rise and fall of the slave power in America*, Boston, 1872, Vol. I, p. 191.
86. *Atlantic Monthly*, August, 1861, Vol. 8, p. 174.
87. *The Southampton Insurrection, op. cit.*, p. 116.
88. "The participation of white men in Virginia Negro insurrections", *Journal of Negro History*, XVI, 1931, pp. 163-164. Chesterfield County is in the Piedmont district.

adjoining countys they all must be in strict readiness, that
this occurance will go throug Virginia with the slaves and
whites if there had never been an association—a visiting with
free and slaves this would never had of been. They are put
up by the free about their liberation. I've wrote to Norfolk
Amelia, Nottoway and to sevel other countys to different
slaves bob and bill Miller Bowler john ferguson—and sevel
other free fellows been at Dr. Crumps—and a great many
gentlemens servants how they must act in getting their liberation they must set afire to the city begining at Shokoe
Hill then going through east west north south Set fire to the
birdges they are about to break out in Goochland and in
Mecklenburg and several other countys very shortly. now their
is a barber here in this place—tells that a methodist of the
name edmonds has put a great many servants up how they
should do and act by setting fire to this town. I do wish they
may succeed by so doing we poor whites can get work as
well as slaves or collord. this fellow edmonds the methodist
says that judge J. F.—is no friend to the free and your Richmond free associates that your master Watkins Lee brocken-
berry Johnson Taylor of Norfolk and several other noble
delegates is bitterly against them all—servants says that billy
hickman has just put him up how to do to revenge the whites—
edmonds says so you all ought to get revenge—every white in
this place is sceared to death except myself and a few others
this methodist has put up a great many slaves in this place
what to do I can tell you so push on boys push on.

Your friend Williamson Mann.

There appears to be no reason to question the authenti-
city of this letter, but to determine its meaning and to evalu-
ate it are difficult. It appears probable that Ben Lee was a
Negro slave, the name Lee coming from his "master Watkins
Lee." This gives meaning to the phrase "edmonds says you
all ought to get revenge." This and other phrases in the letter,
as the one telling of his having written to "different slaves,"
indicates the existence, on how great or small a scale cannot
be said, of a common feeling among the poor, the exploited,
slave or free Negro or white.

But nothing Nat Turner ever said, so far as what he said
is known, would indicate that there was this unity in the
movement he led, and it appears certain that no white people
were concerned with the carrying out of the revolt itself.
The letter does substantiate Floyd's statement about the
existence of a rebellious spirit among some of the poorer
whites, which, as will later be shown, seems also to have
existed in North Carolina, and indicates that this spirit was
aroused by the Turner Revolt. Some results of this will be
observed when the effects of that event are considered.

E: Defeat and Capture

The quick suppression of the Revolt may be explained
by the poor arms and almost, if not quite, total lack of ammunition possessed by the Negroes; the fact that some, apparently, became drunk; all were fatigued; and the separa-
tion of the forces, against the advice of Turner, when on
their way to the county-seat, Jerusalem (now called Courtland); and, at the final test, the superior force and arms of
the whites. It is, however, to be noticed that, notwithstanding the fact that two of the reasons some Negroes hoped for
success were beliefs that the British would aid them and that
there were but 80,000 whites in the country,[89] had Nat Turner been successful in capturing Jerusalem, with its arms
and ammunition, he might have prolonged the conflict for
many days; perhaps, with guerrilla warfare, for weeks.

Mr. R. P. Howison wrote:[90] "But when within a few miles
of the place, (Jerusalem) they were met by a small body of
white men, armed with guns generally loaded *with bird-*

---

89. See letter of E. D. Guion to Thomas Ruffin, *Papers of Thomas
Ruffin,* J. G. de Roulhac Hamilton, editor, p. 45; W. S. Drewry,
The Southampton Insurrection, Washington, 1900, pp. 39-40; The
Atlas, quoting editor of Richmond *Whig,* Vol. 4, p. 7, New York,
September 17, 1831.

90. A *History of Virginia from its discovery,* N.Y. & London, 1848, Vol.
II, p. 441. (emphasis in original).

shot, and at the first discharge, the cowardly wretches turned and fled to the swamps behind them." U. B. Phillips similarly wrote that[91] sixty Negroes were dispersed by eighteen whites, ". . . . armed like themselves with fowling pieces with birdshot ammunition . . . ." But the factors mentioned and soon to be demonstrated sufficiently explain the defeat of the Negroes without resorting to the charge of cowardice; and the example Howison and Phillips select to substantiate that charge is fallacious.

After riding and fighting all Sunday night and Monday morning, Turner brought together his force and started out for Jerusalem. A few miles from that town they passed the gate of the estate of a wealthy farmer, a Mr. Parker. Some of the Negroes wished to recruit his slaves, and over the objections of Turner, set out for the home about half a mile from the gate. Some of those starting out appear to have been under the influence of Southampton cider (it has been mentioned that products of the orchard were important in the economy of the country) and they appear to have taken more refreshments from Mr. Parker's well-stocked cellar. Nat Turner became impatient and, leaving, as he stated, seven or eight men at the gate, went to fetch his tardy followers.[92] It was this handful of slaves which was attacked by eighteen whites and, according to Drewry,[93] who certainly is not sympathetic, the Negroes were armed ". . . . with few rifles, fowling-pieces loaded with bird shot being the general weapon. The negroes were also in want of ammunition and used gravel for shot, Nat insisting that the Lord had revealed the sand would answer the same purpose as lead." This is substantiated by the Richmond *Compiler*[94] of August

91. *American Negro Slavery* . . . . N.Y. and London, 1918, p. 481.
92. *The Confessions,* Thomas Gray, Baltimore, 1831, pp. 15, 16—the fact that seven or eight men were left at the gate is also given by W. S. Drewry, *op. cit.,* p. 62; J. W. Cromwell, *Journal of Negro History,* V, 211, (1920).
93. W. S. Drewry, *op. cit.,* p. 66.
94. Given in *The Atlas,* Vol. III, no. 52, Sept. 10, 1831, N.Y.

29: "They had few fire arms among them—and scarcely one, if one, that was fit for use." This group retreated, but was re-enforced by the returning Turner and his companions. Now the whites retreated, but they, in turn, were re-inforced by a body of militia which dispersed the slaves. Turner, with a much reduced force, appears to have still made sporadic raids, but this engagement at Parker's Field was the critical one and by Tuesday, the 23rd, the Revolt was crushed. Soon three companies of federal troops (which, as previously stated, had been recently stationed at Fort Monroe for this purpose), with a field piece and 100 stands of spare arms with ammunition had arrived, at the request of the Mayor of Norfolk, J. E. Holt.[95]

General Eppes,[96] commanding the forces at Jerusalem, reported to the Governor that he had taken forty-eight prisoners. Other[97] estimates place the number at the low fifties. There is uncertainty, too, as to what was done with these men. The Samuel Warner pamphlet, published a month after the Revolt, gives the names, owners and dates of executions of nineteen slaves, but in the Gray pamphlet, seventeen slaves are given as having been executed (four free Negroes are mentioned as having been sent for further trial; it appears that three of these were hung.) Eight of the Negroes Warner gives as having been hung are listed by Gray as having suffered transportation.[98] The lowest estimate of the number hung is eleven,[99] given by U. B. Phillips, but most

---

95. "Federal Aid in domestic disturbances 1787-1903", H. C. Corbin and F. T. Wilson, *Senate Document* No. 209, 57th Cong., 2nd sess. (Vol. 15), Washington, 1903, p. 56, 261.

96. *The Atlas*, Sept. 10, 1831, Vol. III, No. 52, New York, quoting the Richmond *Compiler* of August 29th.

97. As examples; J. W. Cromwell, *Journal of Negro History*, V. 214; A. B. Hart, *Slavery and Abolition, 1831-41*, N.Y. & London, 1906, p. 218; U. B. Phillips, *American Negro Slavery . . . .* , New York, London, 1918, 481.

98. S. Warner, *Authentic and Impartial narrative . . . .* , New York, 1831, p. 15; T. Gray, *The Confessions . . . .* Baltimroe, 1831, p. 23.

99. *American Negro Slavery, op. cit.*, 481 note 76; J. C. Ballagh says 13, *A History of Slavery in Virginia, op. cit.*, Baltimore, 1902, p. 94.

later[100] accounts follow quite closely that given by Thomas Gray.

Nat Turner successfully eluded his pursuers from the end of August to October 30, when he was caught, armed only with an old sword, by Benjamin Phipps. During those weeks there had been rumors that he was caught, that he was a runaway in Maryland, that he was drowned, but he had never left Southampton.[101] He left his hiding place only at night for water, having supplied himself with food.[102] On November 5, the honorable Jeremiah Cobb pronounced the sentence of the Court,[103] which closed as follows: "The judgement of the Court is, that you be taken hence to the jail from whence you came, thence to the place of execution, and on Friday next, between the hours of 10 A.M. and 2 P.M. be hung by the neck until you are dead! dead! dead! and may the Lord have mercy upon your soul."

And on November 11, 1831, Nat Turner went to his death, calmly and apparently unafraid,[104] in the city of Courtland, then known as Jerusalem, in Southampton County, Virginia. But, though Jeremiah Cobb exclaimed dead! thrice, and even had he so exclaimed three hundred times, Nat then, at the moment of his execution, only began to live.

---

100. As example see A. B. Hart, *op. cit., Ibid.,* J. W. Cromwell, *op. cit., Ibid.*
101. The capture is in *The Confessions,* p. 16; it has been very often, and, on the whole, accurately, retold. For the rumors, see Richmond *Enquirer,* October 18, 1831; *Niles' Weekly Register,* October 29, 1831, XLI, 162.
102. *The Confessions,* 16; in *The Communist,* X, 741, N. Stevens suggests he was given food by Negroes. No evidence of this has been seen.
103. W. S. Drewry, *The Southampton Insurrection,* Washington, 1900, p. 100, note 2, gives the entire sentence. What his source was is not known.
104. See, for example, New York *Evening Post,* November 19, 1831.

THE EFFECTS

When what appear to be the effects of the Nat Turner Revolt are scrutinized, the generalization that may fairly be drawn is that their tendency was to *accentuate existing trends* and thus to help bring about an open and decisive break between the Northern and Southern civilizations. It is true that such factors as soil exhaustion, rivalry in westward expansion, agrarianism versus industrialism, slave versus free labor, were all-important causes of this break, were, indeed, the break itself. But it is also true that such prolonged and objective forces need some overt, subjective, spectacular *event*[1] to crystallize them.

A: TERROR AND MAYHEM

An anxious, nervous, ill-at-ease social order was suddenly hit by a bloody revolt of considerable proportions. What happened? Panic flashed through Virginia accompanied by a reign of terror. The uprising was infectious and slaves everywhere became restless, or, it was feared that they had or might become restless, so the panic, momentarily localized in Virginia, spread up to Delaware and down to Florida, across to Louisiana and up again into Kentucky. The lid which the slavocracy had clamped down upon the press and the rostrums of debate and lecture was blown off and a shiver slid through the South and reached the North. The class economically, politically and socially dominant became alarmed, threw aside pretense, whispers, cant, and openly

---

1. James Truslow Adams has well written: "Events are forces momentarily made visible." *Revolutionary New England, 1691-1776*, Boston, 1923, p. 4.

and defiantly unfurled its flag: No change—we will give not an inch. Repressive laws were passed, vigilante committees and mobs organized, distinguished theorizers in favor of slavery boldly announced their doctrines, the lid was replaced and clamped down and remained down as prosperity of this class returned in ever-increasing volume. The anti-slavery forces in the South, never confident, never sure of themselves, gave ground, spoke first of greater gradualism, of colonization, but shortly even this position was evacuated. Abolitionist societies disappeared from the South and sprang up by the hundreds in the North. The critical period had begun. Try as many did, there was to be no more effective evasion, no more neutrality, no more indifference—one civilization, one type of social organization was now irrevocably pitted against the other.

The first account in the Richmond *Whig*[2] assured its readers that ". . . . no serious danger was apprehended." Somewhat later the *Enquirer*[3] still had a reassuring note, rather refuted by facts given within the reassurance: "Everything is quiet here. Never more so—And indeed it is the same case, in very quarter from which we have heard— No one has dreamed of any such event happening in any part of Virginia—A patrol turns out in our city every night— Our tranquility (sic) is perfectly unrufled (sic)—no disturbance, no suspicion, no panic—not even any excitement, except on account of our brethren of Southampton.—A temporary company of horse is organizing for a patrol, until our two Volunteer Companies (sent to Southampton) return."

A letter from a business man of Richmond,[4] dated August 28, 1831, to the editors of the New York *Journal of Commerce* indicates that tranquillity was gone. This gentleman stated: "We can now conceive that the murders at South-

---

2. Richmond *Whig*, August 23, 1831.
3. Richmond *Enquirer*, August 26, 1831.
4. Given in New York *Evening Post*, September 2, 1831. (emphasis in original).

ampton could not have been so much an affair of runaway negroes, as was at first supposed; and the question now arises, if the slaves in that county, would murder the whites, whether they are not ready to do it in any *other county* in the State; and whether the reports that may spread among the slvaes (sic) in other parts of the States, may not *excite* those to insurrection that never thought of such a thing before." And the sincerity of this person's alarm appears clearly in this passage: "If they attempt any harms in towns, they would most likely resort first to *fire* to aid them: and goods destroyed by such a fire would not be paid for by insurers. For this reason we should not, just at this time, care to have goods sent us on which we might have to make advances." And the letter[5] from Chesterfield County of August 29, 1831 from "Your friend Williamson Mann," previously full given, stating ".... every white in this place is sceared to death ...." further indicates anything but tranquillity.

About two weeks later "A Friend of Precaution" writes:[6] ".... The question is now presented to the mind of every thinking man in the low country, how can a remedy be provided? the safety of our wives and children, and their lives be preserved?" More than a month after this Mrs. Lawrence Lewis in her letter to Harrison Gray Otis, once before referred to, writes:[7] "The dreadful events of August last in our State, the want of confidence and insecurity produced by those horrors, *compel me* to address you." She thinks "Our whites unhappily evince *too much fear* of those wretches .... it is like a smothered volcano—we know not when, or where, the flame will burst forth, but we know that death in the most horrid form threatens us. Some have died, others have become deranged from apprehension since the South

---

5. J. H. Johnston in *Journal of Negro History,* XVI, 164.
6. Richmond *Enquirer,* September 13, 1831.
7. S. E. Morison, *The Life and Letters of Harrison Gray Otis, Federalist 1765-1848,* Boston and New York, 1913, Vol. II, 259-260. (emphasis in original).

Hampton affair." The lady says that she will try not to appear afraid but admits "I cannot feel secure or happy now." She also writes, as did the editor of the Richmond *Whig*: "I have been assured by several Gentlemen who have visited the devoted district, (Southampton) that should the blacks attempt to rise there again, they will be exterminated, the excitement is so great."

The Negroes did not make this attempt but scores were nonetheless "exterminated" within the "devoted district." And, as will later appear, this process of extermination was not confined to Southampton.

Drewry thought:[8] "There was far less of this indiscriminate murder than might have been expected, and as many guilty negroes escaped as innocent ones perished." How much "indiscriminate murder" should be "expected" is not known but the last assertion by Drewry is false and contradicts his own previous estimate of the number of guilty Negroes—sixty or seventy,—because at least that number, as will be shown, were murdered. Ballagh[9] wrote: "A most impartial trial was given to all, except a few decapitated at Cross Keys . . . ." (within Southampton) and Phillips[10] simply noted ". . . . a certain number of innocent blacks shot down. . . . ."

General Eppes' statement[11] leads one to fear that these three historians were quite uncritical in dealing with this phase of the event. ". . . . He (the General) will not specify all the instances that he is bound to believe have occurred, but pass in silence what has happened, with the expression

---

8. W. S. Drewry, *The Southampton Insurrection*, Washington, 1900, p. 86; similar sentiments of Drewry are uncritically quoted by J. E. Cutler, *Lynch Law* . . . . New York, London, Bombay, 1905, p. 95.
9. J. C. Ballagh, *A History of Slavery in Virginia*, Johns Hopkins Un. studies in historical and political science, extra vol. XXIV, Baltimore, 1902, p. 93.
10. U. B. Phillips, *American Negro Slavery* . . . . New York, London, 1918, p. 481.
11. Richmond *Enquirer*, September 6, 1831; mentioned by T. W. Higginson, *Atlantic Monthly*, August, 1861, Vol. VIII, 179.

of his deepest sorrow, that any necessity should be supposed to have existed, to justify a single act of atrocity.—But he feels himself bound to declare, and hereby announces to the troops and citizens, that no excuse will be allowed for any similar acts of violence, after the promulgation of this order, and further to declare, in the most explicit terms, that any who may attempt the repetition of such act, shall be punished, if necessary, by the rigors of the articles of war. The course that has been pursued, he fears, will in some instances be the means of rendering doubtful the guilt of those who may have participated in the carnage, ... This course of proceeding dignified the rebel and the assassin with the sanctity of martyrdom, and confounds the difference that morality and religion makes between the ruffian and the brave and honorable." The editor of the Richmond *Whig*[12] also referred "with pain" to this "feature of the Southampton Rebellion . . . . We allude to the slaughter of many blacks without trial and under circumstances of great barbarity." He did not know how many were thus killed but thought that no more than forty would be correct.[13]

A Reverend G. W. Powell,[14] writing on August 27, 1831, reported ". . . . *many negroes are killed every day*: The exact number will never be ascertained." The Reverend was correct, but it is probable that a good many more than forty were killed. The *Southern Advocate*[15] reported that over one hundred Negroes had been killed in Southampton, and Samuel Warner declared:[16] "The number of Blacks slain is sup-

---

12. Quoted in the *Atlas*, New York, Sept. 17, 1831—Vol. IV, p. 6; see also a letter to same effect in New York *Evening Post*, September 5, 1831.

13. Benjamin Lundy also thought "some thirty . . . . were put to death without trial . . . ." *Life, Travels and Opinions of*— . . . . , Philadelphia, 1847, p. 246.

14. The *Liberator*, (Boston) Vol. I, p. 155, Sept. 24, 1831. (emphasis in original).

15. *Southern Advocate* (Huntsville, Alabama,) October 15, 1831, quoting Edenton, (N.C.) *Gazette,*—as does *Liberator*, Oct. 22, 1831, Vol. I, p. 170.

16. *Authentic and impartial narrative* . . . . , N. Y. 1831, p. 15.

posed to amount to more than One Hundred." This estimate is followed by some[17] secondary accounts but obviously only the crudest approximation is possible. It appears safe to say that at least as many Negroes were killed without a trial as whites had perished due to the Revolt and that probably the number in the former case was considerably more than in the latter.

While and after this was going on in Southampton County there were rumors of plots and of revolts among whites and Indians, as well as Negroes, and often imprisonments and lynchings and executions in the rest of Virginia, Maryland, Delaware, North Carolina, South Carolina, Alabama, Louisiana, and Tennessee and terror in every state south of the Susquehanna.

These events were not calculated to restore complacency or prestige to a type of society finding it difficult to maintain itself. Naturally, then, one of the main props, generally speaking, of any social order, the press, was not likely to report them faithfully or fully. Niles stated: "There have been many executions in Virginia and North Carolina, and some, we believe, in other states—about which little has been said in the public papers." Indeed, somewhat earlier, he had himself written: "We have prepared what may be regarded as something like a *history* of the late insurrectionary movements among the slaves in North Carolina, with some account of the effects of them—but it *must* be postponed."[18] And was, permanently. Yet considerable material may be obtained from the press and from other sources.

Very early one may read of the conviction of ten or eleven Negroes in three eastern counties of Virginia, one in

---

17. *Race Relations*, W. D. Weatherford, C. S. Johnson, New York, 1934, 272; *The National Cyclopaedia of American Biography* . . . . New York, 1906, XIII, 597; A. B. Hart, *Slavery and Abolition 1831-1841*, (Vol. 16 of *American Nation* series), New York and London, 1906, p. 218.
18. *Niles' Weekly Register*, (Baltimore,) Nov. 18, 1831, XLI, 221; Oct. 1, 1831, XLI, 74.

Nansemond, one in Prince George and eight or nine in Sussex. A day later the arrest and subsequent release of twelve in Norfolk and the arrest and conviction of one in Fredericksburg and the jailing of forty more in Nansemond County are reported.[19] The Richmond *Compiler*[20] of September 3, 1831, contains this item: "Some rumors are still afloat; but we know not on what authority they rest, and we hope they are very much exaggerated; as, of a deposit of guns, pistols, and knives, being found in Nansemond—though a late letter from that county says all alarm had subsided. Yet we now and then hear of a suspected slave taken up in Nansemond and Surry—and we hear a report of a Patrol going upon an estate in Prince George—and upon the overseer's pointing out five whom he suspected, shooting two who were attempting to make their escape, and securing the other three and throwing them into jail."

Other items illuminate the terror in Virginia. Reports were current that there were two or three thousand Negroes

---

19. *Ibid*, Sept. 24, 1831, p. 67; *Richmond Enquirer*, Sept. 20, 1831; *National Intelligencer*, Washington, Sept. 21, 1831. A table on population in *contiguous counties of Southampton* will help explain the most severe case of contagion.

Population 1830.

COUNTY	WHITES	SLAVES	FREE NEGROES
Greensville	2104	4681	332
Isle of Wight	5023*	4272	1222
Nansemond	5143	4943	1698
Surry	2865	3378**	866
Sussex	4118	7736	866

These figures are from *Documents containing statistics of Virginia ordered to be printed by the state convention* . . . . 1850-51, Richmond 1851, no pagination—see tables headed "The Census—A Tabular Statement," etc.,
   *Drewry and Weeks incorrectly give this as 7023—the *Southampton Insurrection*, 109 note 1; *Magazine of American History*, XXV, 454 n.
 **Drewry has 3377, *ibid*; *Niles' Weekly Register*, XLIII, p. 30, Sept. 8, 1832 has this as 3376. He also gives the total number of free persons in Surry as 3831;—3731 is correct; See also *American Annual Register* 1830-31, p. 381; J. H. Hinton, et al. *History and Topography of U.S.* . . . . , Boston, 1846, p. 443.
20. Quoted in Richmond *Enquirer*, September 6, 1831.

in the Great Dismal Swamp[21] (in Southampton County and extending into North Carolina). Five "full and efficient volunteer companies have been formed, or renewed at Petersburg," and a letter from Brunswick County stated all were under arms.[22] The Negroes imprisoned in Sussex caused further concern for on October 20th, they attempted to escape.[23] One succeeded, one was killed, "another severely wounded—the remainder were secured without injury. On Friday (October 21) four of them were hung in pursuance of the previous sentence of the Court." There is evidence[24] of killing in another eastern county: ". . . . in Charles city county, a rising of the negroes being feared, an armed body of white men shot down two blacks, because they attempted to run away. There is much *fear* and *feeling* in several of the lower counties of the state, and the white inhabitants seem to be in a constant excitement."

The following letter,[25] probably written in December, 1831 or January, 1832, graphically portrays the terror that gripped many of the citizens of Virginia. "A gentleman in Virginia thus writes to his friend in this city. (Cincinnati). 'These insurrections have alarmed my wife so as really to endanger her health, and I have not slept without anxiety in three months. Our nights are sometimes spent in listening to noises. A corn song, a hog call, has often been a subject of nervous terror, and a cat, in the dining room, will banish sleep for the night. There has been and still is a *panic* in all this country.

"'I am beginning to lose my courage about the meliora-

---

21. *Niles' Weekly Register*, XLI, 35, Sept. 17, 1831; (S. Warner) *Authentic and impartial narrative* . . . . N.Y., 1831, p. 12.
22. *Niles' Weekly Register*, XLI, 35; New York *Evening Post*, August 29, 1831.
23. New York *Evening Post*, November 1, 1831.
24. *Niles' Weekly Register*, XLI, 19, September 10, 1831. (emphasis in original).
25. The *Liberator*, Vol. II, p. 14, Jan. 28, 1832, quoting Cincinnati *Journal* (n.d.) (emphasis as here given)—Yet W. S. Drewry wrote "By December, 1831, all alarm had passed away . . . ." *The Southampton Insurrection*, p. 160.

tion of the South. Our revivals produce no preachers; churches are like the building in which they worship, gone in a few years. There is no principle of life. *Death is autocrat of slave regions.'*"

The people of Delaware and Maryland, too, were terrified. A paper[26] of October 4 reports ". . . . several negroes imprisoned in Georgetown, Del. . . . ." and 24 jailed in Sussex, Delaware. Two weeks later[27] excitement is reported in Easton, Maryland, and a "rising" in Seaford, Maryland. A few days later this appears: "Agitations. The lower part of the state of Delaware and the adjacent parts of the Eastern shore of Maryland, have been much agitated by apprehensions of a servile insurrection, and a good many persons of color were arrested—many expresses sent off for arms and men, and awful reports were heaped upon one another by fear! *There does not appear to have been the least foundation for this excitement*—but the ease with which it was *worked up* shews a most unhappy state of society. The manufacturers of news killed one whole family—who, it seems, were amazed at finding themselves dead—in the papers." Samuel Warner's pamphlet[28] states: ". . . . strong symptoms were manifested by the Slaves in Maryland and Delaware to revolt . . . ." A later account refers to "slaves to be hung in Delaware."[29]

The terror in North Carolina was at least equally widespread and the immediate results appear to have been bloodier. And, in this state, it is interesting to note that it was thought the ". . . . extensive and organized plan to bring about desolation and massacre . . . . it may be awfully believed, was not altogether confined to slaves. . . . "[30]

In a postscript to a letter from Chowan County, writ-

---

26. Richmond *Enquirer*, October 4, 1831.
27. *Niles' Weekly Register*, XLI, 141. (emphasis as in original).
28. *Authentic and impartial narrative. . . .*, New York, 1831, p. 26.
29. The *Liberator*, Vol. I, p. 170, October 22, 1831.
30. *Niles' Weekly Register*, XLI, 80, October 15, 1831.

ten by Thomas S. Hoskins to Judge Thomas Ruffin, is one of the earliest reports of the trouble in North Carolina. It is dated Edenton, N.C., September 2nd, 1831 and, in part states:[31] "The Guard and Patrol are very strict everywhere. The jails are filled to overflowing. Ten likely fellows were bro't to town last night and put in jail, from the upper part of this County, C. E. Johnson's and Genl. Brownrigg's etc. Proof is *said to be* strong vs. them. Many people are up night and day." A news report of September 17th declares,[32] ". . . . *it is said* that troops were marching for Newbern, N.C. where an insurrection was expected, or had actually broken out; and it is well known that the white people in all this section of the country are arming themselves, and that suspicion and fear prevails to an unprecedented extent." As a matter of fact troops had already been sent to Newbern, Captain F. Whiting commanding one company, which had taken along a field piece.[33] Niles[34] gives the contents of a letter from Raleigh, of September 13, to a Mr. Barnum in Baltimore ". . . . saying that expresses had arrived announcing that *Wilmington was in the hands of the blacks and burnt!*—that it was reported they *were marching on Raleigh*—that the citizens had been all night under arms—and the women, almost distracted, were flying all directions. All business was stopped, except in preparation for events. At the instant of writing an express arrived from *Johnson County* (this is properly spelt Johnston) (adjoining that in which Raleigh stands), demanding arms and ammunition! Wilmington *was* (must we say?) a large town, and had a great commerce." But the next edition

---

31. *The papers of Thomas Ruffin,* collected and edited by J. C. de Roulhac Hamilton, Raleigh, 1918, pp. 47-48. (emphasis in original).
32. *Niles' Weekly Register,* Sept. 17, 1831, XLI, 35.
33. "Federal Aid in domestic disturbances 1787-1903", H. C. Corbin and F. T. Wilson, *Senate documents,* 209, 57 Cong, 2d sess., (Vol. 15) pp. 56, 262-263.
34. *Niles' Weekly Register, op. cit., ibid.;* see also W. S. Drewry, *The Southampton Insurrection,* 154; J. W. Cromwell, *Journal of Negro History,* V. 215.

declared that this was false,[35] that panic caused the report and that martial law had been declared in Raleigh with all free Negroes being subjected to questioning. The press of the 20th of September had more rumors of plots and revolts. It was said there was an uprising in Duplin County of two hundred Negroes and[36] that, "There never was such excitement in Sampson and Duplin before." Ten or fifteen Negroes were in jail in the former county and two had been executed in the latter.[37] And "The Raleigh Star of[38] Thursday last says —'We understand that about 21 negroes have been committed to jail in Edenton, on a charge of having been concerned in concerting a project of rebellion. . . . .'" On September 23rd an attempt was made to lynch four Negroes in Wilmington (New Hanover County). One escaped but "three ringleaders of the late diabolical conspiracy, were executed. . . . ."[39] Although the Fayetteville *Observer* of the 21st lamented the fact that rumors gained such easy currency, the press[40] three days later reported fears of insurrection in that very city. A paper of October 4, reported the execution of four Negroes in Wilmington who, according to a later report by Garrison, were first flogged until they "confessed."[41] This same writer reported plots among the Negroes in the gold mines of Rutherford and Burke Counties.[42] On October 19 was reported the conviction of seven more Negroes, three in Duplin, three in Pitt and one in Richmond Counties, and ten days later it was stated that forty-six Negroes were imprisoned at Union and some in Spartanburgh, Greenville and Lincolntown. There was also, at this time, reported the

35. *Niles' Weekly Register,* XLI, 67, September 24, 1831.
36. New York *Evening Post,* September 20, 1831.
37. Richmond *Enquirer,* Sept. 20, 1831; *National Intelligencer,* (Washington), Sept. 21, 1831; H. M. Wagstaff, *State Rights and Political Parties in North Carolina, 1776-1861,* Baltimore, 1906, p. 57-58.
38. *National Intelligencer,* Sept. 21, 1831.
39. *Ibid.,* October 5, 1831.
40. New York *Evening Post,* Sept. 24, 1831.
41. Richmond *Enquirer,* Oct. 4, 1831; The *Liberator,* Oct. 15, 1831.
42. *Liberator, ibid., Anti-Slavery Manual,* LeRoy Sunderland, N.Y. 1837, p. 90; W. S. Drewry, *op. cit.,* 152.

imprisonment of four whites for maliciously circulating false rumors.[43]

Here is a not untypical paragraph from a Fayetteville, North Carolina paper of November 9, 1831, as quoted in the New York paper, *Infidelity Unmasked*, January 14, 1832:

> We learn that during the sitting of the Superior Court of New Hanover, last week, seven negro men slaves, concerned in the late conspiracy, were found guilty and sentenced to be hung in Wilmington. . . . One other slave was sent to Duplin county, there to be tried; and three free men of color were being tried at the date of our last information. The Superior Court of Sampson County is in session this week. A considerable number of negroes is to be tried.

In the Warner pamphlet[44] mention was made of the execution, after flogging, of four Negroes in Sampson County. A paper of November 25, reported the execution of six more Negroes in Wilmington, and also contained an account of the conspiracy of a Negro named Fed, which has previously been mentioned.[45]

Bassett stated:[46] "I have it on the authority of the son of the man who was at that time sheriff of Sampson County that the negroes executed for this crime there were innocent, and that he had often heard his father say as much." Something tending to confirm this appeared in a contemporary paper.[47] "A letter of late date from Fayetteville, on this subject, says that the whole state (North Carolina) has been thrown into alarm by the exaggerated reports of persons who have related as facts what was suggested by their fears. The writer sums up the truth of the matter in a few words: 'There

---

43. New York *Evening Post*, Oct. 19 and Oct. 29, 1831.
44. (S. Warner) *Authentic and impartial narrative* . . . . N.Y. 1831, p. 25.
45. Richmond *Enquirer*, November 25, 1831.
46. J. S. Bassett, *Slavery in the State of North Carolina*, Baltimore, 1899, Johns Hopkins Un. Studies, XVII, (7-8), p. 97.
47. *National Intelligencer*, Washington, Sept. 24, 1831. (Word in bracket added by present writer.)

has not been a single (White) person in the State injured
—there has not even been a rising.'"

Fear created suspicion, suspicion led to torture, torture
to confessions. Or, it is possible, and that is but a guess, that
the panic, or part of it, was maintained by people interested
in the purchase of slaves at a low price. Another hypothesis
was suggested by Bassett:[48] "It would be interesting to know
whether or not these frights were of political origin." Probably all ideas help explain the terror. Much of the panic was
groundless, perhaps some stirred up for selfish reasons and
probably there were rebellious movements on the part of
some of the Negroes and poorer whites in North Carolina.

The fear pervaded Alabama and South Carolina also.
Higginson[49] is correct in pointing to Governor Hayne's proc-
lamation "to prove the groundlessness of the existing alarms
as indicating at least the prevalence of such alarms." Henry[50]
stated, ". . . . in Laurens district two slaves were tried and
convicted of being in an agreement to meet others and to
join in such an undertaking [revolt] if the opportunity should
arise." A letter[51] from Fort Mitchell, Alabama, October 3,
1831, written by one J. Clay to Gen. Lowell Woolfolk, in-
tendant of the town of Columbus, tells of fears of revolt
of Negroes aided by Indians. There is also an extract of a
letter,[52] dated October 26, 1831, from Alabama to a gentleman in Boston: "We are in a great state of alarm, in consequence of an attempted rising of the slaves here. Many
have been arrested, and are now undergoing trial; what the
final result will be, I cannot say—my own impression is, that

---

48. J. S. Bassett, *op. cit.*, 97; Similarly, C. H. Ambler suggested that
    Calhoun and his press agent, Duff Green, exaggerated the extent of
    the abolitionist propaganda in order to unite the South and get the
    Presidency. *Thomas Ritchie* . . . . Richmond, 1913, p. 167.
49. T. W. Higginson, *Atlantic Monthly*, Aug. 1861, Vol. VIII, 181.
50. H. M. Henry, *The police control of the slave in South Carolina*,
    Emory, Virginia, 1914, p. 153.
51. The *Liberator*, October 29, 1831.
52. *Ibid.*, November 26, 1831, quoting the "Morning Post," see also
    T. W. Higginson, *op. cit., ibid.*

the infection is pretty general with the negroes throughout the country. The sedition, however, is hushed for the present." Hushed so well, indeed, that no hint of anything like this appears in the Alabama papers consulted.

There are further indications that the fear was real and widespread. Olmsted told of his[53] conversation, in the late fifties, with two poor whites of Mississippi. " 'Where I used to live, (Alabama) I remember when I was a boy—must ha' been about twenty years ago—folks was dreadful frightened about the niggers. I remember they built pens in the woods where they could hide, and Christmas time they went and got into the pens 'fraid the niggers was rising.' "

" 'I remember the same time where we was in South Carolina', said his wife, 'we had all our things put up in a bag, so we could tote 'em, if we heard they was comin' our way.' "

Georgia and Tennessee also were disturbed. The *Messenger*[54] of Macon, Georgia apologized ". . . . for the barrenness of the present paper" and offered as an excuse the fact that its staff was on patrol duty. In Tennessee there was report of the discovery of an actual conspiracy in Fayetteville. "Their object was to set fire to some building, and amidst the confusion of the citizens, to seize as many guns and implements of destruction as they could procure, and commence a general massacre. Many of those, who were engaged in this infernal conspiracy, have been *slashed with the severity which the iniquity of their diabolical schemes, so justly deserved.*"[55]

---

53. F. L. Olmsted, *A journey in the back country*, London, 1860, p. 203; quoted by U. B. Phillips, *American Negro Slavery* . . . . New York, London, 1918—who believed correctly, that this referred to time just after the Turner Revolt, p. 483.

54. *The Liberator*, October 22, 1831; referred to by T. W. Higginson, *op. cit.*, 181.

55. *Niles' Weekly Register*, XLI, 340, Jan. 7, 1832, quoting *The Western Freeman*, Shelbyville, Tenn. (emphasis in Niles'); *Anti-Slavery Manual*, LeRoy Sunderland, second edition, N. Y., 1837, p. 89; T. W. Higginson, *op. cit.*, 181, referred to a plot in Louisville, Kentucky—this has not been seen elsewhere.

Evidences of the great uneasiness in Louisiana before the Turner Revolt have been presented. One may, then, expect this event to have produced much commotion in that state, and it did, but precise information has not been found. But the concern here was great enough to be one of the reasons for the early convening of the State Legislature by Governor A. B. Roman.[56] The Governor stated in his message of November 14, 1831, that rebellious activities in Louisiana could be but "momentary" but he declared: "These insurrections have, with much reason, excited the serious attention of most of the states of the south. They have taught the necessity of adopting effective measures for preventing the like scenes of disorder; and we cannot be astonished that here perhaps more than any where else, they have been regarded with most needful anxiety."

The reports of revolts in Brazil, Tortola and, particularly, in Jamaica in the last months of 1831 and the early months of 1832 added to the distraught condition of the mind of the slavocracy.

B: LOCAL OR GENERAL

One immediately wonders whether these plots and conspiracies, or any of them, were directly connected with the activities of the Southampton revolutionists. Did Nat Turner, or any of his followers, spread the word and help form plans for other revolts, before he or they revolted? Or are the disturbing movements which followed the Turner attempt to be ascribed to infectiousness, to panic, to imagination,

---

56. The *Atlas*, New York, December 10, 1831, IV, 103; *Niles' Weekly Register*, XLI, 314, Dec. 24, 1831—The early convening was also due to a vacancy in the U.S. Senate and to protest against a repeal of the duty on sugar—see previous sources and *American Annual Register*, 1831-32, second edition, 1835, (New York) p. 271. See also T. W. Higginson, *Atlantic Monthly*, VIII, op. cit., 182.

57. The *Liberator*, Oct. 22, 1831; *Niles' Weekly Register*, XLI, 131, 479; LaRoy Sunderland, *Anti-Slavery Manual*, *op. cit.*, 90; R. Coupland, *The British Anti-Slavery Movement*, London, 1933, p. 136.

to political or economic motives? It is believed that no certain answer may properly be made to these questions on the basis of the evidence, but it does appear, on consideration of that evidence, as highly probable that the Turner Revolt was a local affair.[58]

This hypothesis is favored because the widespread terror and unrest, real or supposed, are sufficiently explained by the factors above mentioned. It is, also, to be recalled, as shown earlier in this book, that plots and unrest had been prevalent, or had been believed to be prevalent, in most of the slave states directly *before* the Turner Revolt. Furthermore, the man who was in the best position to answer this question, did answer it, and declared it was local.[59] "I see, sir," he said to Thomas Gray, "you doubt my word but can you not think the same ideas and strange appearances about this time in the heavens might prompt others, as well as myself, to this undertaking?"

The evidence to support the contrary view is not convincing. Wagstaff wrote:[60] "Southampton bordered the North Carolina line, and the wild plot extended over the border among the dense slave population of the contiguous counties." His reference, W. S. Drewry, does present evidence[61] which may be pointed to, to support this statement. But this evidence is based on memory, and it is not clear whether it is meant to show that the terror spread, or, what is here the question, whether the plot was widespread. In fact the evidence he submits is so confused that while

58. This conclusion is stated by some secondary sources—but it is simply stated; there is no consideration of evidence pro or con. See J. C. Ballagh, *A History of Slavery in Virginia*, Extra Vol. XXIV, J. Hopkins Un. Studies, Baltimore 1902, p. 93; W. C. Bryant and S. H. Gray, *A Popular History of the United States*, N.Y. 1881, Vol IV, 321. J. R. Brackett, *The Negro in Maryland* . . . . Johns Hopkins Un. Studies, extra volume VI, Baltimore, 1889, p. 66.
59. *The Confessions*, Baltimore, 1831, p. 17; W. S. Drewry, *The Southampton Insurrection*, p. 152.
60. H. M. Wagstaff, *State Rights . . . in North Carolina, op. cit.*, 57.
61. W. S. Drewry, *op. cit.*, pp. 78-79; 151-160.

Drewry[62] seems to think that the plot was not widespread, he states: "Both of the views are in a measure true." Both cannot in any "measure" be true; either the plot was widespread or it was not.

Governor Floyd accurately said,[63] as has been displayed in some detail, that "There is much reason to believe that the spirit of insurrection was not confined to Southampton . . . ." But were the manifestations of that spirit *planned* in Southampton? According to Samuel Warner,[64] one Negro confessed that Turner had been promised aid from "North Carolina, Maryland, etc." and he believed this because of the "alarming symptoms" the Negroes of those states "exhibited to revolt." The editor of the Richmond *Whig*[65] also mentioned confessions of Negroes pointing to a widespread plot, though he thought, nevertheless, that the plot was "confined to Southampton." The usual method of obtaining these confessions makes one highly suspicious of them.

McSherry thought the plot was not local. He wrote:[66] "The conspiracy of Nat Turner and his associates, in Virginia, had extended its ramifications over a portion of this state; (Maryland) but a misunderstanding about the day fixed for the rising, saved Maryland from the bloody scenes which were enacted in Virginia." No reference[67] was given. Confessions which may have been obtained under torture and the reminiscences of old men about exciting times and

---

62. W. S. Drewry, *The Southampton Insurrection*, Washington, 1900, 155-156—the quotation is from page 155.
63. *Journal of House of Delegates* 1831-32, no pagination—see *Niles' Weekly Register*, XLI, 350, January 7, 1832.
64. *Authentic and impartial narrative* . . . . New York, 1831, p. 18.
65. The *Atlas*, New York, Sept. 17, 1831, Vol. IV. p. 7.
66. James McSherry, *History of Maryland from its first settlement in 1634* . . . . second edition, Baltimore, 1849, p. 358 (cited by J. R. Brackett, *The Negro in Maryland, op. cit.*, p. 96 note 1); in the edition of McSherry edited and continued by B. B. James, Baltimore, 1904, this passage is not to be found notwithstanding the fact that James, in the preface said "everything of the author's has found incorporation, although not always *in situ.*"
67. Probably his source was the editor of the Richmond *Whig*—see his statement in The *Atlas, op. cit., ibid.*

the almost incoherent, arbitrary, statements of a reverend gentleman[68] are not sufficient evidence to explain a series of events, which are, without this hypothesis, perfectly understandable.

C: FRENZIED LEGISLATIVE ACTIVITY

One of the important and direct results of the Nat Turner Revolt and the terror that followed, was the almost frenzied legislative activity of the slave regions, state, territory, and city. It has been shown that the social unrest of the last half of the second decade resulted in many bills and laws in the slave states aimed against free Negroes and the enlightenment or improvement of the slave. Now the year of terror beginning with the Turner Revolt had similar results. It will be observed that they were of three general groups: (1) repression of the free Negro ("Various severe measures are contemplated against[69] the free people of color. . . . ." "But the public attention . . . . is unfortunately chiefly called to the free blacks."); (2) repression of the slave, ("It is charged against the slaves lately condemned that a number of them were 'preachers of the Gospel'—and[70] that those who had been the most kindly treated and were the best informed, were most prominent. The *bearing* of these remarks is easily seen, and will add to the burthen of the suffering"); (3) attempts at the amelioration of the social unrest, mainly resulting in greater efforts of colonization of the free Negroes and in the repression, or possible repression, of the whites themselves.

The legislature of Delaware of January to February, 1832, enacted laws forbidding free Negroes, under a five dollar fine, from keeping fire-arms without having a license

---

68. Statement of Lorenzo Dow as given by W. S. Drewry, *op. cit.*, 155 note 2. It is a long jumble of almost incomprehensible mutterings. Drewry's reference is simply "Life and Works"—an attempt to check this failed.

69. *Niles' Weekly Register*, XLI, 221, Nov. 19, 1831; XLI, 340, January 7, 1832.

70. *Niles'*, *op. cit.*, XLI, 221, Nov. 19, 1831. (emphasis as in original).

from a Justice of the Peace. A ten dollar fine was the penalty
provided for all meetings of more than a dozen free Negroes,
continuing past 10 P.M., unless these were directed by at
least three white men. And a free Negro, who did not reside
in the State, was not to preach or exhort unless he had a
license from a Justice of the Peace, under a penalty of fifty
dollars. Provision was made, also, requiring licenses for the
entering or temporary withdrawal of slaves.[71]

Brackett accurately remarked:[72] "The year 1831 is a
landmark in all legislation in Maryland affecting the negro,
slave and free." But the structure he displayed as this landmark is quite incomplete. The General Assembly of Maryland
of December 26, 1831 to March 14, 1832 made the following
pertinent laws: The immigration of free Negroes was forbidden. The unlucky person of that description in Maryland
more than ten days was to pay a fine of fifty dollars a week.
None of these newly arrived Negroes was to be given any
employment. No free Negro was to have any arms. Slaves
and free Negroes were permitted to have religious services
only with whites. No foodstuff or tobacco was to be bought
from any Negro, and no one was to sell spirituous liquors to
any Negro, nor was the latter to sell any to anyone. The
importation of slaves, *for sale*,[73] after June 1, 1832 was forbidden. The Maryland State Colonization Society was incorporated and a Board of Managers, of three persons, was
to be appointed by the Governor and Council. This Board
was to spread propaganda about Liberia and to remove free

---

71. In part in *Laws of the State of Delaware from the sixteenth day of
January* . . . . , published by S. Kimmey, Dover, Vol. VIII, 1841, pp.
279-280; C. G. Woodson, *The Negro in our History*, fifth edition,
Washington, 1928, p. 186; *American Annual Register, 1831-32*, sec-
ond edition, *op. cit.*, 1835, p. 253; *Niles' Weekly Register*, XLI, 479,
Feb. 25, 1832.

72. J. R. Brackett, *The Negro in Maryland, op. cit.*, p. 66.

73. Laws of this type were early and often passed and were always dead
letters—in North Carolina, 1794-1800, 1802, 1803; Maryland, 1796;
Delaware, 1787, 1789; Kentucky, 1815; Georgia, 1817; Louisiana
1826, 1829—G. M. Stroud, *A Sketch of the laws relating to slavery*
. . . . second edition, Philadelphia, 1856, pp. 88 ff.

Negroes from the state. Twenty thousand dollars were given for 1832 and permission to later borrow up to $200,000 ($200,000 was *not*[74] "appropriated"). If not enough Negroes volunteered to leave to use up the money gotten, force was to be used. Moreover, a resolution was passed, the preamble of which was: "Whereas, recent occurrences in this state, as well as in other states of our Union, have impressed more deeply upon our minds, the necessity of devising some means, by which we may facilitate the removal of the free persons of color from our state . . . ." our Congressmen are asked to get the aid of the national treasury, and, if necessary, to amend the Constitution so that this can be done.[75]

The lawmakers of North Carolina also earnestly tried to earn their pay, although they had passed so many laws in 1828 and 1829 that not much remained to be done. But at the session of 1831-1832 a law was passed forbidding free Negroes and slaves to preach or exhort under a penalty of 39 lashes.[76] The slave was not to exercise his (or her) own time in employment at his own discretion. A free Negro who had been fined but could not pay his fine was to be sold as a slave at auction to that person agreeing to take him for the shortest time. It was also provided that, at the request of five justices, the Governor was to issue a commission of oyer and terminer to speed up the trials of slaves accused of insurrection. Finally, an act was passed for the better provision of arms for and the more efficient service of the state militia.[77]

---

74. As said by *Niles' Weekly Register* quoting Maryland *Republican*, XLII, 93, April 7, 1832.
75. *Laws made and passed by the General Assembly of the State of Maryland* . . . . 1831 . . . . 1832, Annapolis, 1832—no pagination—see Chapters 281, 323 and resolution number 124 of 1831.
76. See J. W. Moore, *History of North Carolina from the earliest discoveries* . . . . Raleigh, 1880, Vol. II, 31, (cited by W. S. Drewry, *op. cit.*, p. 170 n. 2).
77. *Acts passed by the General Assembly of the State of North Carolina* . . . . 1831-1832, Raleigh, 1832, pp. 7, 10, 11, 25, 34-36, a few are cited by H. M. Wagstaff, *State Rights* . . . . *in North Carolina, op. cit.*, p. 58 note 80.

The legislative results in South Carolina were meager, though there was discussion of the Revolt by[78] the Governor in one of his messages. The only restrictive legislation was against the making or selling of spirituous liquors[79] by free Negroes in December, 1831. However, the Vigilance Society of South Carolina offered $1,500 on September 29, 1831, for the arrest and trial of any person who published or circulated seditious literature.[80]

Georgia bore its crop of laws, too. The assembly of November and December, 1831 forbade a slave from hiring himself out during his own time (if he had any) and he was not to live away from his owner or manager when in the capital, Millidgeville,[81] or in the counties of Burke, Jefferson, Scriven, Richmond, and Hancock. Georgia also passed a law prohibiting the introduction of slaves for sale.[82] The assembly passed a resolution offering $5,000 for the arrest and trial of the publisher, editor, or any circulator of the *Liberator* or of "any other paper, circular, pamphlet, letter or address of a seditious character,"[83] which moved Niles to comment: "We regret the state of society which should have deemed a proceeding of this sort necessary to its preservation."

The legislative council of the Territory of Florida of January 2, 1832 to February 12, 1832 declared, ". . . . if any person or persons, shall excite an insurrection or revolt of slaves, or shall attempt by writing, speaking, or otherwise, to excite an insurrection or revolt of slaves, he, she, or they, so offending, shall on conviction thereof suffer death." The

---

78. *Acts and Resolutions of the General Assembly of the State of South Carolina* . . . . December 1831, Columbia, 1832,—see section "Legislative Proceedings," p. 13, House of Representatives.
79. *Ibid.*, section of laws—p. 13, Chapter 3.
80. H. M. Henry, *The police control of the slave, op. cit.*, p. 156.
81. *Acts of the General Assembly of the state of Georgia passed in Millidgeville* . . . . November and December, 1831, Millidgeville 1832, pp. 174-75, 223-24, 226-27.
82. *Niles' Weekly Register*, XLI, 267, December 10, 1831.
83. *American Annual Register*, 1831-32, second edit., N.Y. 1835, p. 267.

killing of a slave in revolt was declared to be justifiable homicide. This same act put through a regulation, similar to that of North Carolina, allowing a free Negro unable to pay his fine, to be sold as a slave for the lowest time bid at auction.[84] According to Garrison,[85] writing May 5, 1832, a law was passed "the last year" in Florida increasing patrols, forbidding gathering of three or more slaves unless for "ordinary labor," except if two or more "respectable white persons" were present.

An Alabama newspaper in its number[86] first reporting the Southampton revolt asked: "From the contemplation of this ruffian violence and ruthless destruction, would it not be well to look to ourselves? Are we entirely exempted from all dangers of a like visitation—and ought we not to take some precautions to guard against its possible occurrence? We know that this is a delicate subject and requires delicate dealing, but it ought to be looked boldly in the face." With this example, and the further stimulation of feared outbreaks at home, previously noted, Alabama enacted many laws. These laws, as Lundy stated, were put through by ". . . . the Legislature of Alabama alarmed by the Southampton insurrection. . . . ."[87]

He who attempted to teach any Negro to spell, read or write was to be fined not less than $250 nor more than $500, and "persons circulating or publishing pamphlets, etc., tending to produce insurrection among the slaves shall suffer death." It was declared illegal for five male slaves to congregate off their plantation without the master. No free Negro was to settle in Alabama in 1832, under the penalty of 39 lashes for the first offense, to be sold as a slave thereafter.

84. *Acts of the Legislative Council of the Territory of Florida passed* at the 10th session . . . . Tallahassee, 1832, p. 64; in part—G. M. Stroud, *A Sketch of the laws relating to slavery*, 2d edit., Philadelphia, 1856, p. 27.
85. The *Liberator*, May 5, 1832, Vol. II, p. 70.
86. *The Southern Advocate* (Huntsville, September 10, 1831).
87. *Life, Travels and Opinions of Benjamin Lundy* . . . . Philadelphia, 1847, p. 257.

Free Negroes were not to trade or associate with slaves without written permission from the master. Slaves were not to be introduced for sale. All imported 30 days before the passage of the act were to leave not more than 30 days after.[88] Moreover, the law prohibited ".... the sale, hiring or mortgaging of slaves carried in the State (under the exceptions of the law) (i.e., as brought in by owner, administrator, etc.) for the space of three years .... To illustrate the effect of this law we observe that since its passage, a sale of ninety negroes took place on the 1st ult. in Tuscaloosa, and brought the sum of $41,031.50. They had been appraised by competent judges at half the amount, and would not, it is supposed have brought more but for the late law."[89]— which may help explain the abundance of such laws. Alabama also passed a "noble experiment" law fining cruel masters $500, but its enforceability was nil.[90]

The Assembly of Mississippi of 1831-32 decided that all free Negroes from 16 to 50 years of age were to leave the state within 90 days, though persons of "good character" might get a revokable license to stay. Negroes were not to peddle outside an incorporated town, nor were they to preach, being liable if they did to 39 lashes. The master was, however, permitted to have a preacher for his own slaves. No spirituous liquor was to be sold to a slave without the master's permission.[91]

Features[92] of one of the important laws passed at the extra session of the tenth legislature of Louisiana, as the requiring of a certificate for incoming slaves and an appro-

---

88. G. M. Stroud, *A Sketch of the laws, op. cit.,* 142; *The American Annual Register,* 1831-1832, 2d edit., N.Y., 1835, 268-269.
89. The *Atlas,* New York, Vol. IV, p. 191, February 25, 1832, quoting the *"Milledgv. Record"* (Millidgeville, Georgia?) no date.
90. *The American Annual Register, op. cit.,* 269.
91. *A digest of the laws of Mississippi comprising all the laws* .... T. J. Fox Alden and J. A. Van Hoesen, New York, 1839, pp. 769-771; *The American Annual Register, op. cit.,* 270; the regulation on liquor was repealed in 1833.
92. *Acts passed at the extra session* .... *state of Louisiana,* New Orleans, 1831, p. 140.

priation of $5,000 to enforce this have been mentioned. Although the Governor advised this legislature to totally prohibit the introduction of slaves for a number of years because[93] "after the events that have recently occurred, we have even another danger to apprehend, it is the introduction amongst us of slaves who have participated in the insurrection or conspiracies attempted in other states," it decided to forbid the introduction of slaves for sale, and to prohibit the sale of slaves otherwise brought in for five years after their entrance. The circulation of written material inciting discontent among the free Negroes or insubordination among slaves was a capital offense. Speech of a similar nature made one liable to 3 to 21 years imprisonment and teaching slaves to read or write was punishable by one to twelve months imprisonment.[94] The City of New Orleans[95] required "that any one introducing or bringing slaves in the city, shall within 24 hours after his and their arrival, report the same to the Mayor, accompanied by a statement, upon oath of the sex, age and place, whence each slave was brought, previous to the introduction into this state." And, as will be shown, prices rose, slaves poured in, and Thomas Dew won the day, historically a brief day.

On December 16, 1831, the State of Tennessee forbade the entrance into that state of free Negroes, and declared that slaves were not to be emancipated unless they left the state. Further, "all assemblages of slaves in unusual numbers or at suspicious times and places not expressly authorized by the owners, shall be held and considered an unlawful assemblage." The law of 1741 providing death, or any lesser punishment, for conspiracy to rebel was reaffirmed, and no appeal was to be granted in cases of actual rebellion. How-

---

93. The *Atlas*, New York, Vol. IV, 103, December 10, 1831.
94. *Niles' Weekly Register*, Vol. XLI, 267, Dec. 10, 1831; *Life, Travels and Opinions of Benjamin Lundy* . . . . Phila., 1847, p. 255.
95. New York *Evening Post*, Nov. 4, 1831, quoting the New Orleans *Bee* of October 20, 1831.

ever, slaves and free Negroes were no longer to be punished by having their ears cut off, or nailed to a pillory.[96]

A bill to forbade the importation of slaves as merchandise passed the House in Kentucky in 1831 but was not acted upon by the Senate.[97] But the next legislature, on February 2, 1833 passed a law allowing the importation of slaves only for settlement, not for sale, and requiring an oath to that effect within 30 days of importation.[98] A letter from "A Citizen of Ohio" expressed gratitude that the "township trustees" of Cincinnati "will in future execute the above mentioned laws (requiring bond from immigrating free Negroes) with rigor." The writer does this because "Peculiar circumstances attending the insurrections in the South have made it necessary" that we avoid a poverty-stricken Negro population.[99]

As is to be expected, however, the state where the most momentous legislative activity occurred was Virginia, itself. The least important phase of this activity is the laws that were actually passed. It was provided that ". . . . no slave, free negro or mulatto, whether he shall have been ordained or licensed, or otherwise, shall hereafter undertake to preach, exhort or conduct, or hold any assembly or meeting, for religious or other purposes, either in the day time, or at night," under a penalty of not over 39 lashes. Whites, however, were allowed to take Negroes to their own services and a licensed white preacher was allowed to preach to Negroes during the daytime. No free Negro was to possess arms. If any Negro

---

96. All these regulations may be found in *Public Acts passed at the stated session of the nineteenth general assembly of the State of Tennessee, 1831,* Nashville, 1832, pp. 121-123; parts in *The American Annual Register* 1831-32, 2d edition, N.Y., 1835, p. 273; B. Brawley, *A Social History of the American Negro* . . . . N.Y. 1921, p. 148.
97. *American Annual Register, op. cit.* 275; N.Y. *Evening Post,* December 5, 1831.
98. *Acts passed at the first session of the forty-first general assembly for the Commonwealth of Kentucky* . . . . Frankfort, 1833, pp. 258-259.
99. The *Atlas,* New York, Vol. IV, 79, Nov. 19, 1831; a similar step was announced in 1829, see E. S. Abdy, *Journal of a residence and tour in the United States* . . . . London, 1835, Vol. III, pp. 10-11.

should commit assault on a white person with intent to kill, death without benefit of clergy was to be his punishment. No one was to sell liquor or to purchase it from a slave and no Negro was to sell liquor within one mile of a public assembly. Any Negro assembling at a seditious meeting or saying or writing anything of such a nature was to be lashed not over 39 times, a white to be fined from $100 to $1,000. This act[100] went into operation July 1, 1832.

Another act,[101] passed March 5, 1832, ". . . . though," as the printer, Thomas Ritchie, stated, "applicable to one county only, is deemed sufficiently important, (as affecting the general policy of the state), to be inserted among the acts of a public nature," legalized the proceedings of a public meeting in Northampton County where $15,000 were pledged for the colonization of free Negroes. This sum was to be part of the debt of the county.

But what this legislature did not do, and why it did not do these things, and what various citizens inside and outside the honorable body thought it ought to do and why, and what was said to and in, and reported about and asked of this body are of greater significance than the laws it passed. Yet before discussing these things a question suggests itself when all the laws and regulations passed as a result of the stirrings of 1831 are given. Was the condition of the slave worsened or not?\The information needed to answer this question has not yet been brought together and very little is definitely known about the comparative standards of living of slaves in different regions and different periods (or, for that matter, of other inhabitants). But there is some testimony that should warn the wary against assum-

---

100. *Acts passed at the general assembly of the commonwealth of Virginia* . . . . December . . . . 1831, Richmond 1832, pp. 20, 21, 24; in part in J. C. Ballagh, *A History of Slavery in Virginia*, Johns Hopkins Un. Studies, Extra volume XXIV, Baltimore, 1902, p. 93.

101. *Acts passed at the general assembly, op. cit.,* p. 23; see *Slavery Agitation in Virginia,* 1829-1832, T. M. Whitfield, Johns Hopkins Studies, Extra volume, new series, No. 10, Baltimore, 1930, p. 114; J. C. Ballagh, *op. cit.,* 147.

ing that since repressive slave laws entered the statute books at a given period, that period saw a declining standard or condition of existence for the slaves.

True, as the laws[102] would indicate, and as Moore[103] stated, worship by the Negro slaves themselves was for a number of years stopped. It is also true, as Andrews stated,[104] and, again, as the laws would indicate, that the terror did lead the white rulers ". . . . to remove from the slave, so far as it was practicable, every element of power. Hence has resulted a more fixed determination to keep him in ignorance, for 'knowledge is power.'" These and other factors Miss Martineau acknowledged,[105] but yet thought ". . . . they are substantially better treated; they are less worked by hard masters; less flogged; better fed and clothed. The eyes of the world are now upon the American slave and his master: the kind master goes on as he did before, the hard master dares not be so unkind as formerly." And here again some of the laws previously given would substantiate this. Olmsted,[106] writing in the middle fifties, quoted a gentleman of Virginia as having ". . . . considered the condition of slaves to have much improved since the Revolution, and very perceptibly during the last twenty years." /The laws enumerated do, however, strongly suggest, and no extenuating evidence is known, that the free Negroes were severely hit by the wave of repression which started in about 1829 and got its greatest stimulus from the revolt of 1831.

D: THE VIRGINIA LEGISLATURE, 1831-32

Much has been written concerning what the Virginia

---

102. E. A. Andrews, writing July 17, 1835, thought the Virginia laws of 1831-32 were "dead letters," *Slavery and the domestic slavetrade* . . . . Boston, 1836, p. 60; see also U. B. Phillips, *American Negro Slavery* . . . . N.Y., London, 1918, p. 484.
103. J. W. Moore, *History of North Carolina* . . . . Raleigh, 1880, II, 31.
104. E. A. Andrews, *op. cit.*, p. 197, letter of August 1, 1835.
105. H. Martineau, *Society in America*, 4th edit., N.Y., London, 1837, I, 380.
106. F. L. Olmsted, *A Journey in the seaboard slave states* . . . . (originally issued in 1856) N.Y., London, 1904, I, 108.

legislature of 1831-32 did not do and why it did not do these things, but not very much that is accurate. The former calls for enumeration, the latter discussion.

Several petitions[107] were received asking that Negro apprenticeships in such trades as plasterers, painters, masons, be forbidden, which ". . . . may be deemed indirect or secondary effects" of the Turner revolt and the agitation it produced. A few petitions[108] were presented asking that something be done to solve the "Negro problem." A motion was made (by a Mr. Witches) to postpone consideration of this subject indefinitely.[109] This was voted down, 71 to 60. Since it was to be considered, a select committee on slaves, free Negroes and the revolt was appointed. On Wednesday, January 11, 1832, the chairman of this committee "Mr. Goode of Mecklenburg (Piedmont) rose to move the following resolution:

> *Resolved*, that the select committee raised on the subject of slaves, free negroes, and the melancholy occurrences growing out of the tragical massacre in Southampton, be discharged from the consideration of all petitions, memorials, and resolutions, which have for their object, the manumission of persons held in servitude under the existing laws of commonwealth, and that it is not expedient to legislate on this subject."[110]

The resolution, *as to what the committee ought to do*, brought forth two suggested amendments. Mr. Preston[111]

---

107. T. M. Whitfield, *Slavery Agitation in Virginia, 1829-32, op. cit.*, pp. 119-120.
108. One of these, that from the ladies of Fluvanna County, is very inaccurately given by W. S. Drewry, *The Southampton Insurrection*, Washington, 1900, p. 165 n.—words are altered, and much is omitted, though this is not indicated. See *Niles' Weekly Register*, XLI, 273, Dec. 10, 1831. It is very long, but worth reading.
109. The *Constitutional* (Richmond) *Whig*, January 28, 1832.
110. *Journal of the House of Delegates*, 1831-32, no pagination: this and T. J. Randolph's resolution were printed in full on the first page of the pamphlet of his speech delivered on January 21, 1832 and printed by Thomas W. White, Richmond, 1832 (Virginia State Library).
111. Richmond *Whig*, January 28, 1832.

suggested that "expedient" be substituted for "not expedient," which was defeated 58 to 73, and Mr. T. J. Randolph of Albemarle (Piedmont) ". . . . moved the following substitute to be inserted after the word 'Southampton':— be instructed to inquire into the expediency of submitting to the vote of the qualified voters in the several towns, cities, boroughs, and counties of this commonwealth, the propriety of providing by law that the children of all female slaves, who may be born in this state, on or after the 4th day of July 1840, shall become the property of the commonwealth, the males at the age of twenty-one years, and females at the age of eighteen, if detained by their owners within the limits of Virginia, until they shall respectively arrive at the ages aforesaid, to be hired out until the nett sum arising therefrom, shall be sufficient to defray the expense of their removal, beyond the limits of the United States, and that said committee have leave to report by bill or otherwise." This never came to a vote.[112]

On January 27, Gen. W. H. Brodnax, of Dinwiddie (Piedmont) from the same committee,[113] reported a long bill, the purpose of which was colonization of the free Negroes. He was careful to explain that nothing would be done which might be damaging to the security or value of private property. It provided for the appropriation of $100,000 for the current year and $200,000 for succeeding years to be made to a Central Board, composed of the Governor, Treasurer, and Executive Council, which might form subsidiary boards in strategic cities, as Norfolk, Petersburg, etc. If not enough free Negroes to use up the appropriation volunteered, force was to be used. This recommended bill was amended by the House so that $30,000 were to be expended

---

112. See note 110 ante.
113. In the bound volume called the *Virginia Slavery Debate of 1832* in the Virginia State Library there is an appendix by Brodnax explaining his colonization bill; and see his speech of January 19—printed by Thomas White, Richmond, 1832; see also Richmond *Whig*, January 28, 1832.

the first year and $90,000 the next year, and the clause making provision for the colonization of Negroes freed with no money provided by their masters for their transportation was stricken out. This last action adversely affected the western vote and the bill, though passing the House, was defeated in the Senate by a close vote.[114]

As has been remarked the Southampton revolt precipitated the legislative debate under consideration; it, as a contemporary newspaper correspondent aptly[115] remarked, was ". . . . the touch of the rock which called the waters forth." It is then important here to examine the claim that this debate and the discussion it brought forth demonstrated that Virginia was ready or nearly ready for abolition. The failure to accomplish this is very often[116] ascribed to the irritating activities of the abolitionists, who are dragged in by these writers to explain away any distasteful condition. They will ascribe the Turner revolt to the abolitionists, implying that only in that way can one explain a revolt of dear old Virginia Negroes, and then explain the anti-slavery utterances made by Virginia legislators four months later by saying that abolitionist agitation had not then really begun. But when the Virginia legislature accomplishes nothing, the abolitionists are again dragged in to account for this failure.

---

114. The vote seems to have been 18 to 14—see the Richmond *Whig* of March 12, 1832 and *Niles' Weekly Register* XLII, 78, March 31, 1832. A tradition has arisen that this bill was beaten by one vote— See *The Virginia Magazine of History and Biography*, XI, (1904) Richmond, p. 331, where Brodnax's emasculated bill is called one for "abolishing slavery"!; *The Old Free State*, L. C. Bell, Richmond, 1927, I, 496; E. Channing, *A History of the United States*, N.Y. 1921, V. 144; B. B. Munford, *Virginia's Attitude toward slavery and secession*, N.Y., London, 1909, p. 46.

115. Richmond *Enquirer*, March 3, 1832.

116. There are almost innumerable examples: B. B. Munford, *op. cit.*, 48, 41-59; B. H. Wise, *The life of Henry A. Wise of Virginia 1806-1876*, N.Y. 1899, p. 46; *Mr. Buchanan's administration on the eve of the rebellion* (by Buchanan) N.Y., 1866, pp. 3-4; T. N. Page, *The Old South* . . . . N.Y., 1892, p. 38; H. A. Herbert, *The Abolition Crusade* . . . . N.Y., 1912, pp. 12, 61 ff; G. T. Curtis, *Life of James Buchanan*, N.Y., 1883, II, 278-279; L. P. Stryker, *Andrew Johnson* . . . . N.Y., 1929, p. 50.

A factor very closely associated with this question is the change in the enunciated ideology of Virginians which set in immediately after the lid of repression had been pried open by the sword of Nat Turner. But, while this is related, it is distinct and, for the sake of clearness, will be, as much as possible, treated separately. The fact is that the statements and activities of the honorable members themselves and of writers in newspapers and pamphlets are sufficient proof that, at the end of 1831 and the early months of 1832, emancipation was not wanted by the rulers of Virginia, by the slaveholders.

Jesse Macy thinks the opposite and states that this debate shows[117] ". . . . that the traditional anti-slavery sentiment still persisted among the rulers of the old Dominion." The traditional lip-service perhaps, though even that was beginning to decline. And, it was never more than that. Miss Adams[118] writes: "Virginia, it is claimed by many, would have abolished slavery if a longer time had been allowed her. If that statement is true, there must have been a decided change after 1831. Up to that time the majorities through her whole history seem to be really on the side of slavery." There was a change after 1831; a swing to vehement denunciation of even any *talk* of emancipation.

True, the Richmond *Enquirer*[119] painted a dark picture and shouted "something must be done," and pointed, in terror, at the disproportionate growth of the Negro population, and alarmed some, like Mr. Nathan Alexander,[120] who canceled his subscription and asked that the paper be boycotted. True, the Norfolk *Herald* exclaimed:[121] "Heavens!

117. *The Anti-Slavery Crusade,* (Chronicles of America, V. 28), 1921, New Haven, p. 62.
118. A. D. Adams, *The Neglected period in anti-slavery agitation,* N.Y., London, 1918, p. 54.
119. Richmond *Enquirer,* January 7, 1832; referred to by H. Martineau, *Society in America,* 4th edit., N.Y., London, 1837, I, 361; G. Weston, *The progress of slavery in United States,* Washington, 1857, p. 200.
120. Richmond *Enquirer,* January 12, 1832.
121. Quoted in Richmond *Whig,* January 17, 1832.

shall we fear the consequences of a public investigation of the evil with a view to its gradual removal, and not shudder at the inevitable results of permitting it to grow upon us?" But what, concretely, what did the *Enquirer* suggest? "In fine, by *great discretion, the utmost respect for private property, great perseverance, by an active and increased police,* we may rid ourselves, in some long and distant times of an evil, which, if left to itself, will 'grow with our growth, and strengthen with our strength,' "[122] This is the high point in "emancipationist" feeling in this eastern Virginia newspaper, and it is difficult to ascertain whether the writer is deploring slavery, or asking that its too rapid growth be checked. W. S. Jenkins[123] appears to be, in general, correct when he states that at this period, that is during the terror following the revolt, and before the return of prosperity for the slaveholders, (i.e., from about September 1831 to about April 1832) ". . . . to many Virginians, the evils of slavery were beginning to outweigh the benefits, and, instead of coming forward to defend slavery as a good, they remained reticent and sought some ameliorating scheme, not that they would have abolished the institution, but that they would have eradicated the evil and most dangerous elements attendant."

But it is a mistake, and a very common one, to believe that at this time there were no defenders of slavery per se. Letters and articles did abound giving all the anti-slavery arguments that were to be repeated for a generation; it ruins the land, drives out white laborers, causes immorality, is contrary to our republican institutions.[124] But the other type of letters, now being considered less pretty, are

---

122. Richmond *Enquirer*, January 19, 1832 (emphasis in original); yet L. P. Stryker writes: "The Richmond *Inquirer* (sic) urged that slavery be abolished." *Andrew Johnson, op. cit.,* p. 45.
123. W. S. Jenkins, *Pro-Slavery thought in the old South,* Chapel Hill, N. C., 1935, p. 82.
124. Richmond *Enquirer,* Nov. 4, 1831; Dec. 10, 1831; March 3, 1832; Richmond *Whig,* Jan. 19, 1832; Jan. 21, 1832.

passed over by evaluators of public opinion. One individual "A Slaveholder and No Politician," wrote,[125] in part: "Some people seem very anxious to devise some scheme for the gradual emancipation of our slaves; if they knew what was good for themselves they had better let that question rest; for as I live, *for one*, they will have to take them at the point of the bayonet. I do not mean to go into a discussion of the subject, but merely to state that public sentiment is against *any scheme* of emancipation." And there is the letter from one Richard Hughes telling[126] of the decision of his neighbor, one Colonel Lee, to free his slaves and hire white men: ". . . . they'll be cheaper, he says: and he can make more money on his plantation than he does now. Colonel, says I, the white laborers must be better fed, and clothed, and lodged, than your negroes—and you'll have to pay them wages too; — how can you make more money then? But the negro children he says—the white men will have their children, too, says I; and if you think they can work harder than the blacks, I reckon you'll be out—for no people will work more, or ought to work more than our negroes do— they'll do their work well too, if the master or overseer be good for anything—but this last I didn't say to him." And, as a final example, there is this delightfully frank letter from "A. B. C. of Halifax City":[127] "This one thing we wish to be understood and remembered,—that the Constitution of this State, has made Tom, Dick and Harry, *property*—it has made Polly, Nancy, and Molly, *property;* and be that property an evil, a curse, or what not, we intend to hold it. Property, which is considered the most valuable by the owners of it, is a nice thing; and for the right thereto, to be called in question by an unphilosophical set of political mountebanks, under the influence of supernatural agency or deceit, is insufferable."

125. Richmond *Whig*, January 28, 1832 (emphasis in original).
126. Richmond *Enquirer*, March 1, 1832.
127. Richmond *Whig*, April 13, 1832 (emphasis in original); see also unsigned letter in Richmond *Enquirer*, Feb. 9, 1832.

Much the same may be said of the oratory within the legislative hall. Slavery was denounced, vigorously, vehemently; but by whom? by the *rulers* of Virginia? No, by the western members, those who had, vainly, sought for equal political power just a year before.[128] They represented a region which felt itself, justifiably, deprived of political power and found that the instrument used by the east to do this was slave property. Moreover, at this time not only was this political fact present and the social difference present, but economically, there was little tie between the two sections. J. A Chandler[129] said, speaking of the Virginia of 1830: "The intercourse was so poor that in going from the eastern to the western portion of the State one was often compelled to go through Maryland and Pennsylvania. West Virginia trade went to Baltimore." Some eastern members, as Brodnax, Randolph, Henry Berry, denounced slavery[130] and even declared themselves for ". . . . future gradual emancipation . . . ." but as a western member, Charles J. Faulkner,[131] said of Gen. Brodnax's colonization plan: "Its spirit is pacific—its purpose is compromise. But sir, like most propositions, which, in stormy and tempestuous times, seek conciliation rather than any decisive result or policy—which address themselves more to good feeling than to our enlightened judgement—I fear it deals too much in contradictions and seeks too fancifully to reconcile impossibilities."

While it is, then, true that the general sentiment of the debate was that slavery was an evil, it is not true that it was not here defended in itself. This idea probably has its origin

---

128. See, H. von Holst, *The Constitutional and Political History of the United States*, (J. Lalor transl.) Chicago, 1879, II, I, 58; G. M. Weston, *The Progress of Slavery in the United States*, Washington, 1857, p. 201; C. H. Ambler, *Sectionalism in Virginia* . . . . Chicago, 1910, p. 192; W. S. Jenkins, *Pro-Slavery thought, op. cit.*, p. 87.
129. *Representation in Virginia*, Johns Hopkins . . . . studies . . . . Number 14, 6-7, Baltimore, 1896, p. 45 note 2.
130. The quotation is from the speech of Henry Berry on Jan. 20, 1832, p. 4, Richmond, 1832; W. H. Brodnax, Jan. 19, 1832; T. J. Randolph, Jan. 21, 1832.
131. Speech of Jan. 20, 1832, Richmond, 1832, p. 13.

in statements made by two members[132] of the legislature itself stating that. But one member said:[133] "I have been astonished to find that there are advocates here for slavery, with all its effects. Sir, this only proves how far, how very far, we may be carried by pecuniary interest. . . ." At least three are known to have defended Negro slavery. One was John Thompson Brown of Petersburg,[134] speaking January 18, whose defense was founded on the assumption referred to in the beginning of this work; the innate inferiority of the Negro and the impossibility of his improving himself. Mr. Brown further felt that the decline of Virginia was not so great as it had been painted and that what decline had occurred was due more to the tariff than to slavery. But Brown did not defend "slavery in the abstract." However, both W. H. Roane and W. D. Sims on January 16 and January 26 defended it per se.[135]

Furthermore, as appears from the account of the proceedings previously given, there was no bill or resolution favoring emancipation which was put forward for action *by the assembly* itself, notwithstanding the fact that Marquis James[136] not only states that such a procedure did occur but feels himself even able to explain why it failed; ". . . . because the people did not wish the free blacks on their hands." Randolph's plan was offered for consideration by a committee and that was beaten. W. C. Bruce[137] stated that his ancestor, Charles Bruce, who voted against Gen. Brodnax's colonization bill in the Senate regretted it ". . . . for if the proposition had been carried, the curse of slavery would have been lifted from the back of Virginia, she would have refused to secede from the Union . . . ." which would have

132. Speech of C. J. Faulkner, *op. cit.*, p. 17; speech of W. Preston, Jan. 16, 1832, in Richmond *Enquirer* of Feb. 9, 1832.
133. Speech of Henry Berry, *op. cit.*, p. 2.
134. Pamphlet of that speech printed by Thomas White, Richmond, 1832, pp. 24-26.
135. W. S. Jenkins, *Pro-Slavery Thought, op. cit.*, pp. 86-87.
136. *The Raven, a biography of Sam Houston*, N.Y., 1929, p. 374.
137. *Below the James, a plantation sketch*, N.Y., 1918, pp. 152-153.

spared blood and treasure. Edward Channing[138] tended to agree: "Whether the scheme would have worked out as its promoters believed it would can only be a matter of surmise, but one excellent observer, Charles Bruce of Charlotte County, Virginia, expressed his opinion and that of many other Virginians that had the Colonization Bill of 1831 not been defeated, as it was by a single vote [sic, see note 114 ante] the fire that lurked in the slavery question would have been drawn off by redoubled exertion on the part of the Virginia anti-slavery men, and that, if this had so fallen out, Virginia would not have seceded in 1861. Confirmatory of this general view is the opinion of D. R. Goodloe that had the abolition plan carried in Virginia, it would have been repeated in North Carolina." Here Channing was using colonization plan and abolition plan synonymously which is, of course, erroneous. No abolition bill was submitted, and one very gradualistic emancipation proposal was not even submitted to committee.

The colonization bill as it passed the House was modeled on the law of Maryland, previously given, and was no more thorough, but in that state in the three years[139] 1832, 1833, and 1834, but 219 Negroes were sent to Africa at an expense of approximately $16,000. May one not, then, fairly say that referring to Brodnax's colonization bill as an "abolition plan," or believing that it might have done away with slavery in Virginia is ridiculous? And, as will later be shown, there is much reason to doubt that the end of slavery was the motive of those who, in Virginia and anywhere else, favored colonization.

Those who favor the hypothesis here held to be false have not made use of one excellent piece of contemporary evidence which strengthens their idea. The editor of the Richmond *Whig*[140] believed that the following conclusions were

---

138. *A History of the United States, op. cit.,* V, 144-145.
139. J. R. Brackett, *The Negro in Maryland* . . . . Johns Hopkins Un. Studies . . . . Extra Volume VI, Baltimore, 1889, p. 239.
140. January 28, 1832, Richmond *Whig,* (all emphasis as in original).

to be drawn from the assembly of 1831-1832: "1, That it is not expedient at this session, to legislate on abolition. 2, That the colored population of Virginia, is a great evil. 3, That humanity and policy in the *first place*, demand the removal of the free, and those who will become free, (looking to an extensive voluntary manumission). 4, That this will absorb our present means. 5, (undeniable implication), That when public opinion is more developed; when the people have spoken more explicitly, and the *means* are better devised, that it is expedient to commence a system of abolition."

But this was published on January 28 and within a few days disillusionment set in. By January 31, the measure which "humanity and policy" favored and which would "absorb" the means of the state, was denounced because of the coercion feature within it.[141] "The old difference between *meum and teum*." Referring to the opposition offered to Randolph's proposition the editor went on: "Property must be held sacred—property in human beings who are to be born years hence, though it has no present basis upon which even the imagination can rest it, must be held sacred and inviolable.—A proposition to interfere with it, is met by furious indignation, and a threat to stand by their arms— but the rights of free negroes, their constitutional vested rights to liberty and locomotion, without the pretense of any conduct on their part which has merited deprivation, are coolly and violently taken away, before even the passion occasioned by the other proposition had time to subside! If this be not straining at a gnat, and swallowing a camel, we should like to know what is." With propositions 3 and 4 gone, what has become of 5? By March 12 this appears: ". . . . all things relating to the free negroes, except in so far as a change may be effected by the police bill, remain *in statu*

---

141. As a matter of fact the measure was denounced for that, and because, it was said, it would raise the price of slaves, by this editor as early as January 13, 1832—a most erratic editor. Perhaps the newly acquired and, as it turned out, shortly lived freedom of expression went to his head.

quo ante bellum. All goes for nothing, a ridiculous *finale,* all things considered."[142]

E: IMPACT

But was it really ridiculous? No, it was perfectly rational and completely understandable action on the part of the rulers of Virginia. White Virginians seem often to have been what may be called parlor emancipationists. "Yes, yes, isn't it too bad? But what is to be done?" appears to have been polite conversation over the Virginia dinner tables. And when, in the late twenties the fare on this table became rather scanty it appears that an answer was actually desired, and rather bold denunciators of slavery were yet welcomed at this table. But when, a little later, terrified people, long doubting what possible advantage slavery was to them if others had the slaves, demanded concrete things embellished with all the once respectable phraseology, the situation was different. Now the fare and, indeed, the dining room furniture were threatened. Is it expedient to legislate or not? Should Negro apprenticeship be forbidden? These were questions offered not as polite introductory remarks or as a salvage when conversation had lapsed for too long a period. These had a different ring and expected definite answers—and got them—"no," no in every case. And when, by 1833, scanty meals no longer threatened, this "no" was rationalized, and he who, whether "reasonably" or unequivocally, questioned that rationalization was a traitor to Virginia, to the South and to the Nation. The event which, in Virginia, put insistence and urgency into those questions, and made the objections to slavery obstreperous, instead of whispered, was Nat Turner's revolt.

A newspaper correspondent[143] writing of Nat Turner ex-

---

142. Also in *Niles' Weekly Register,* XLII, 78, March 31, 1832.
143. Letter signed "Pamunkey" in Richmond *Whig,* March 30, 1832; the speech of James McDowell, Jr. of Rockbridge, Jan. 21 was very similar—printed by Thomas White, Richmond, 1832. (emphasis in original).

claimed: "His force was augmented wherever he went, and although commencing 'at a late hour of the night,' before the sun rose on his abominable deeds of blood, upwards of sixty of our fellow citizens were launched into eternity!! And now, what evidence have we, that if this attempt had been made in any other part of the State, the success would not have been as great? Are these facts calculated to lull us into security? . . . . Is it wise, is it safe, any longer to hug the adder to our bosoms, when we see that he only awaits an opportunity to pierce us with the sting of death? . . . Is the Legislature bound by the will of the people, or by the will of the *wealthy?* . . . . Although it may be fairly proven, that our peace and tranquillity, and even the security of our lives, require the adoption of some plan to remove this sorest of evils—and although to do this, *facts* big with horror are related—yet, at every step which we take, to effect this high and righteous purpose—at every advance, we are met with the cry of Property! Property! Property!" This in a Virginia paper; indeed it is "most astonishing and miraculous."[144] As Benjamin Watkins Leigh,[145] the leader of the eastern forces in the constitutional convention of 1829-1830, asked in amazement and alarm: "Who could have anticipated, that the bloody horrors of the Southampton massacre, instead of suggesting plans for stricter discipline, would give birth to schemes for emancipation?"

W. S. Jenkins has shown that,[146] in the middle 1820s, slavery was defended, at times, as a good in itself only in the most southern of the slave states, like Georgia and South Carolina and that, "pro-slavery thought in the lower South was unquestionably far in advance of pro-slavery opinion" in Virginia. Yet it is to be noticed that it was only "by 1833

---

144. Speech of W. Preston, Jan. 16, in Richmond *Enquirer,* Feb. 9, 1832.
145. *Letter to the people of Virginia by Appomattox,* Richmond *Enquirer,* Feb. 4, 1832. This was printed as a pamphlet by Thomas White, Richmond, 1832.
146. *Pro-Slavery Thought in Old South . . . . op. cit.,* pp. 71 ff; quotations are from pp. 81 and 77.

the two leading Charleston papers (The Courier and Mercury) were contending that the South was ready to justify slavery as a social benefit." A paper[147] in Alabama in 1831 quoted in full and with no dissenting comment an article from a Virginia newspaper starting, "It is not now a novel or debateable proposition that slavery is a great moral and political curse."

The Turner Revolt had, then, "made the issue acute,"[148] and the champion of the newly aroused slavocracy was Professor Thomas Roderick Dew, whose work appeared in 1832.[149] Although one excellent contemporary critique[150] of this work has apparently been overlooked by Dew's commentators, there has been no dearth of the latter, and their statements appear to be correct. Dew gave the historical argument, and the anthropological one, maintaining that the Negro was an inferior being and that freedom was "something which he cannot comprehend. . . ."[151] The main argument has been well given by Whitfield:[152] "On the one hand, the magnitude of the property involved precluded the possibility of any plan of abolition entailing compensation. On the other their sacred respect for property rendered impossible every scheme that involved confiscation, whether partial or complete. Little matter that men, women, and children had perished and might do so again any day, slaves were property." There was,[153] moreover, a note of reassur-

---

147. *The Southern Advocate* (Huntsville) Oct. 29, 1831, quoting Lynchburgh *Virginian.*
148. A. O. Craven, *Edmund Ruffin* . . . . N.Y. & London, 1932, p. 107; also 125.
149. *Review of the debate in the Virginia Legislature,* T. White, Richmond, 1832, often reprinted, most conveniently in The *Pro-Slavery Argument* . . . . Charleston, 1852; L. P. Stryker gives its date of appearance as 1835 which helps his argument that abolitionist propaganda stopped emancipation, but the date and argument are incorrect; *Andrew Johnson* . . . . N.Y. 1929, p. 50.
150. W. Jay in *Quarterly Anti-Slavery Magazine,* N.Y. April 1836, pp. 211-227.
151. *Pro-Slavery Argument, op. cit.,* p. 460.
152. T. M. Whitfield, *Slavery Agitation in Virginia 1829-1832, op. cit.,* Baltimore, 1930, p. 142, also 140.
153. T. R. Dew, in *Pro-Slavery Argument, op. cit.,* 361, 362.

ance to the slaveholders themselves. He pointed out that all the laws recently passed restricting the slave trade would become "dead letters," for there were ". . . . so many plans which will effectually defeat all these preventive regulations, that we may consider their rigid enforcement utterly impracticable; and moreover, as the excitement produced by the late insurrection in Virginia, dies away, so will these laws be forgotten. . . ." Indeed, as he did not fail to point out, ". . . . wonderful to relate, Virginia slaves are now higher than they have been for many years past. . . ." Ah, there was a wonderful thing indeed!

It is true that in the number[154] of the *Liberator* first noticing the Revolt, appeared this sentence, "If we have been hitherto urgent, and bold, and denunciatory in our efforts,— hereafter we shall grow vehement, and active with the increase of danger." And, while it is difficult to find any increased sharpness in Garrison's paper after the Revolt (if, indeed, it is possible to imagine such an increase) as compared to the paper of the month preceding, it is true, of course, that the Revolt did give the abolitionists, and moderates, a text which may be illustrated by this sentence:[155] "Insurrections are the natural and consequent productions of *slavery*—experience has proved this in all ages and in all nations where slavery has existed. Slavery *ought* to be, *must* be, and shall be abolished in these United States."

But several months later abolitionist letters, pamphlets and speeches were still permitted in Virginia. Weston's words[156] are full of wisdom: "No man is ever restrained from ever pursuing a course in harmony with his own wishes and opinions, merely because he is advised to it by others; although it is common enough, to make the manner of disagreeable advice, the pretext for the purpose, already pre-

154. The *Liberator*, Vol. I, 143, September 3, 1831.
155. The *Liberator*, October 22, 1831, quoting Westfield *Phoenix* (n.d.)
156. G. M. Weston, *The Progress of slavery* . . . . Washington, 1857, p. 184.

determined, to disregard it." The approximate price of a prime field hand in Virginia in 1825, 1826, 1827, 1828, and 1829 was $400. In 1830 it started up slowly and reached about $425. In 1831 it reached $460 and by 1832 was at $500; that is, a rise of 25% in about three years, and it kept going up steadily until 1837 when it hit about $1,100.[157] This rise in prices due to "the increased demand for slaves[158] in the south-western states" and ".... improved methods of agriculture .... better means of inter-communication ...."[159] and the employment given negro slaves upon works of internal improvement and in factories revived the economic interest in negro slaves in the east" (of Virginia). Olmsted[160] also referred to the steady advance in the value of slaves since 1832 in Virginia and went on to express his doubts that the abolitionists were the true cause of the failure of emancipation in Virginia: "It certainly is a curious coincidence—and it can hardly be thought a mere coincidence, it seems to me—that the general indisposition to emancipate slaves has been very closely proportionate to the expense, or loss of cash property, which would attend it."

It is incorrect to say,[161] "The 'irrepressible conflict' was begun—begun by reformers." Rather it seems correct to say[162] ".... resentment at northern interference .... as being more chivalrous, is the reason alleged in public debates, and in newspaper paragraphs." Did not Mr. Green of Culpeper County speak truthfully when, in the Virginian constitutional convention,[163] on October 27, 1829, he said: ".... all

157. U. B. Phillips, *American Negro Slavery* .... N.Y. & London, 1918, table opposite p. 370; also in his *Life and Labor in Old South*, Boston, 1931, p. 177.
158. E. A. Andrews, *Slavery and the domestic slave trade*, Boston, 1836, p. 180.
159. C. H. Ambler, *Sectionalism in Virginia* .... Chicago, 1910, p. 187.
160. F. L. Olmsted, *A Journey in the Seabord slave states* .... (issued first in 1856) N.Y. & London, 1904, pp. 316, 317.
161. L. P. Stryker, *Andrew Johnson* .... N.Y., 1929, p. 50.
162. E. A. Andrews, *op. cit.*, p. 180.
163. *Proceedings and debates of the Virginian state convention* .... Richmond, 1830, p. 64.

men, when acting, especially in large bodies, are governed
by a feeling of interest, and do with little or no scruple,
whatever they suppose their interest to be. I consider it as
a self-evident proposition"?

Governor Hammond's "moral suasion" statement is fairly
well known,[164] but it so nicely puts the matter that quoting
from it, in part, cannot be resisted. He remarks about the
bitterness of the words of the slaveholders and of the abolitionists and to the latter says: "But if your course was
wholly different—if you distilled nectar from your lips, and
discoursed sweetest music, could you reasonably indulge the
hope of accomplishing your object by such means? Nay,
supposing that we were all convinced, and thought of Slavery precisely as you do, at what era of 'moral suasion' do you
imagine you could prevail on us to give up a thousand millions of dollars in the value of our slaves, and a thousand
millions of dollars more in the depreciation of our lands, in
consequence of the want of laborers to cultivate them?"

This shift in stated sentiment may be personalized and
thus concretized by noticing it in certain prominent individuals. Edmund Ruffin early felt that slavery was an evil
and piously hoped that it might gradually, somehow, be
done away with. But he began to seek a definite position
following the excitement consequent on the Turner Revolt
and joyously received Dew's work.[165] By 1835 he was for
slavery and let the world know it. The early attitude of
Thomas Ritchie has been shown by the quotations from his
paper, the Richmond *Enquirer*. Slavery was a curse and
"something must be done." But he, too, soon changed and
by 1835 opposed emancipation, no matter how gradualistic.
The next year he favored Van Buren only on ascertaining

---

164. "Hammond's Letters on Slavery," (1845) in *Pro-Slavery Argument*
. . . . Augusta, 1860, pp. 140-141; quoted by G. M. Weston, *The
progress of slavery, op. cit.*, pp. 185-186; A. B. Hart, *Slavery and
Abolition* . . . . N.Y. and London, 1906, p. 233.
165. A. O. Craven, *Edmund Ruffin* . . . . N.Y. & London, 1932, pp. 108-
109.

that he was "sound" on slavery and by 1839 he was a rabid pro-slavery expansionist.[166] Similarly, the editor of the Raleigh (N. C.) *Register*, Joseph Gales, in 1816 was outspoken against slavery. In 1825 he still felt it was an evil but was uncertain about what should or could be done. By 1830 he thought anti-slavery agitation was "seditious" and by 1835 he was securely aboard the bandwagon of outspoken pro-slavery propagandists.[167] Again, James K. Paulding in 1816 published material denouncing slavery, but by 1836 he had published strong pro-slavery sentiments.

One of the things this change in expressed sentiment involved was a restriction on the liberties of those against the dominant thought. One of the first instances of this occurred in Virginia at the height of the excitement produced by Turner. It appears that some time in September, 1831, a Mr. Robinson, in Petersburg, expressed the opinion that while he deplored the revolt, the slaves did have, in the abstract, a right to freedom. This gentleman was maltreated by a mob of about 100 people, stripped and forced thus to walk to Richmond. The friend of Mr. Robinson, Mr. Carter, at whose house the former had been staying, was also forced to leave the city. "A more open violation of law and contempt of justice, in broad day-light, one rarely meets with; strange, indeed, that we should *ever* meet with it, in this republic! Not the least disgraceful feature in the case was, that the civil authorities, though appealed to, declined interfering."[168]

The many laws restricting freedom of the press and speech have been given and the story of the fight over petitions in Congress and the use of the mails is well known.

---

166. C. H. Ambler, *Thomas Ritchie* . . . . Richmond, 1913, pp. 164-188, 222.
167. J. S. Bassett, *Slavery in the State of North Carolina*, Johns Hopkins Un. studies . . . . Series XVII, No. 7-8, Baltimore, 1899, pp. 100-101.
168. The quote is from R. D. Owen in the *Free Enquirer*, September 24, 1831, III, 388; the account in The *Liberator* of the same day, I, 155, is very full also. A. B. Hart, *Slavery and Abolition, op. cit.*, p. 236, gives the date of this incident as 1832. (emphasis in original).

While this solidified the South, it added to the ranks of the
abolitionists in the North and helped nationalize and sec-
tionalize, the slavery question. No more vacillation: "Resolved, That slavery, as it exists with us, we deny to be an
evil, and that we regard those who are now making war
upon it, in any shape, or under any pretext, are furious
fanatics or knaves or hypocrites; and we hereby promise
them, upon all occasion which may put them in our power,
the fate of the pirate, the incendiary, and the midnight assassin."[169] The critical period had begun, "All who are not
with the abolitionists are against them; for silence and in-
action are public acquiescence in things as they are."[170] In
about 1827 there were 130 anti-slavery societies, of which
106 were in the slave states. But, as Lundy stated, speaking
of the Turner Revolt and the terror that followed, "From
the time these events occurred, Anti-Slavery Societies in the
South ceased almost entirely to be formed, and those previously established, soon sank into disuse." And by 1857
there were 1,016 such societies in the North and none in
the South.[171]

The case, then, appears to be that the shift in expressed
ideology was simultaneous with the increased uneasiness of
the slave regions. The stake was greatest in the lower South;
the uneasiness hit that region first; the shift started there.
A revolt hit Virginia, terror spread throughout the South,
and with this threat to Virginia property holdings, the ideology shifted to resist the attack. This change in Virginia,
in part dependent upon the slightly earlier change in the

169. *Anti-Slavery Manual* . . . . LaRoy Sunderland, 2d edition, N.Y., 1837,
     p. 50, by citizens of Camden, South Carolina, 1834—also p. 51.
170. H. Martineau, *Society in America*, 4th edit., N.Y. & London, 1837,
     Vol. I, 390.
171. For the earlier date see H. Wilson, *History of the Rise and fall of
     the slave power* . . . . Boston, 1872, I, 170; the whole thing is in
     Life, Travels and Opinions of Benjamin Lundy . . . . Philadelphia,
     1847, pp. 218, 295, the quotation is from p. 247; Also in L. D.
     Turner, *Anti-Slavery sentiment in American Literature* . . . . , Wash-
     ington, 1929, pp. 47-48.

lower South, reacted upon that region itself and soon, by about 1835, the slaveholding South was "solid;" and solidly arrayed against an increasingly awakening and increasingly hostile North.

A few other events and trends appear to have been caused or influenced by the Turner Revolt. Most have already been touched upon, but they deserve further treatment. First, one of the outstanding features in the economic and political life of Virginia, sectionalism, was strengthened. As Ambler stated:[172] "The general tone in the argument of the western delegates in 1831-32 was quite different from what it had been in the Constitutional Convention of 1829-30. Now they looked upon negro slavery as the greatest evil which could befall them." Not only did they consider it this, which really was not new, but, and this was new, they loudly announced their views. This resulted not only from physical terror, but also from the fear that the laws restricting slave trading which had been passed by many southern states would lead to a swamping of western Virginia by Negro slavery.[173] The following news item will show that R. T. Stevenson[174] did not exaggerate when he said: "A political struggle between the eastern and western counties of Virginia received from the negro rising an accidental but none the less tremendous emphasis": "Division of Virginia into two States:— A writer[175] in the Lexington Virginia *Intelligencer* has been urging at great length upon the attention of the people of that State a project of dividing into two— the line to be run from the top of the Blue Ridge. The Staunton *Spectator* pronounces the reasons substantial and thinks favorably of the plan. The Richmond *Whig* says of it that

---

172. C. H. Ambler, *Sectionalism in Virginia* . . . . Chicago, 1910, p. 192.
173. See speech of C. J. Faukner of Berkeley, Jan. 20, 1832, Richmond, 1832, p. 8; quoted in part by G. M. Weston, *The Progress of Slavery* . . . . Washington, 1857, p. 201.
174. R. T. Stevenson, *The Growth of the Nation 1809 to 1837*, being Volume XII of *The History of North America*, edited by G. C. Lee, Philadelphia, 1905, p. 328.
175. New York *Evening Post*, November 19, 1831.

whenever the measure is submitted to the people, a thing will happen not very common—both sides will vote for it." The Turner Revolt was the eagerly sought excuse to broach a grievance that only a very much more violent event was to resolve.

There are some indications that the Turner Revolt led a number of white people to leave their homes and seek more secure abodes. Niles[176] feared that this would be a movement of considerable proportions, but the contrary seems to be true; however the evidence is exceedingly scanty. A writer in the Petersburg (Va.) *Intelligencer* stated:[177] "Many people feel unwilling to die and leave their posterity exposed to all the ills, which, from the existence of slavery in our state, they have themselves so long felt. Others are unwilling themselves longer to suffer these inconveniences; some of our best citizens are already removing—others will doubtless follow, unless they can see a probability that, at some period, the evil will be taken away." In a letter from Mrs. Lawrence Lewis[178] to Harrison Gray Otis, previously mentioned, the lady, after describing the terror due to the Revolt added that "Mr. and Mrs. Butler, & their lovely son, will go to Louisiana the 1st Novr., I expect and *fear*." No other primary evidence has been found, and the point was mentioned only by Ballagh [179] who remarked that due to the Revolt ". . . . a number of farmers emigrated." The laws, detailed above, which were passed concerning the free Negroes would lead one to expect considerable migration on their part, though the difficulty of this for these people was very great. Only in E. S. Abdy[180] has definite evidence of actual migration been found. He noted that, "About 100 families

---

176. *Niles' Weekly Register*, XLI, 80, October 15, 1831.
177. *Ibid.*, XLI, 266, December 10, 1831.
178. S. E. Morison, *The Life and letters of Harrison Gray Otis* . . . . Boston, New York, 1913, II, 261. (emphasis in original).
179. J. C. Ballagh, *A History of Slavery in Virginia,* Johns Hopkins Un. Studies . . . . extra volume XXIV, p. 93, Baltimore, 1902.
180. *Journal of a residence and tour in the United States* . . . . London, 1835, III, 86.

had lately been driven, by religious intolerance, into the State (Ohio) from North Carolina, where they were prohibited from meeting together to pray."

According to Brawley the Revolt ". . . . made certain the carrying out of the policy of the Jackson administration to remove the Indians of the South to the West."[181] This has been found nowhere else and Brawley gave no reference. Stronger evidence is needed to substantiate it.

Some evidence of the effect of the Turner Revolt on the colonization movement has been presented. The immediate effect was that ". . . . the cause was greatly revived."[182] As the official organ stated:[183] "There is a great, perhaps a general movement of public sentiment in the State of Virginia, as well as in some other States, favorable to the cause of African Colonization. We have heard of several distinguished men in Virginia who have heretofore felt no interest in this cause, perhaps deemed it visionary, whose more mature reflections have placed them among its friends. In the ranks of these, we believe we may now reckon the able Editors of the Richmond *Whig* and Richmond *Enquirer*. A Friend in Richmond writes, 'The Colonization Society is becoming quite popular amongst political men'" The editor of the Cincinnati *American*[184] also felt that Africa ". . . . is their proper home, and their best interests would lead them to it. Happy for them, if the present distress should direct their attention seriously and permanently to the land of their Fathers." And the Governor of Virginia, in his message of December 6, 1831 suggested colonization as worthy of the legislators' attention.[185] The action taken in Maryland and the meager fruits thereof have been mentioned, as have the

181. B. Brawley, *A social history of the American Negro*, N.Y., 1921, p. 148.
182. E. L. Fox, *The American Colonization Society*, 1817-1840, Johns Hopkins Un. studies . . . . series XXXVII, no. 3, Baltimore, 1919. p. 92.
183. *The African Repository and colonial Journal*, Washington, 1832, Vol. VII, November 1831, p. 281.
184. Quoted in the *Atlas* (N.Y.) November 19, 1831, Vol. IV, 79.
185. *Niles' Weekly Register*, XLI, 350, Jan. 7, 1832.

actions of Northampton County, Virginia and the Virginia legislature. Southampton County itself aided 200 free Negroes to emigrate in 1831.[186] In 1832 a Junior Colonization Society[187] was formed in Virginia and through its efforts the legislature of that state passed, on March 4, 1833, a law appropriating $18,000 a year for the sending of free Negroes to Liberia. Prior to 1830 the receipts of the American Colonization Society had never reached $20,000; that year they exceeded $26,000 and ". . . . by 1834, they mounted to $51,-662.95." But in that very year ". . . . thousands of dollars were due" and nothing was in the treasury. The movement then declined, and this, plus the 1837 panic, brought the receipts down to $11,597 in 1838.[188]

E. L. Fox makes the point[189] that since the colonization bill failed to become a law in Virginia (Brodnax's bill) and since the process of law making was controlled by the eastern members, the slaveholders, it is incorrect to believe, as did Garrison, that the movement was a creature of the slaveholders. But the fact is, as shown, that the bill did pass the House and was defeated by a close vote in the Senate due to the united opposition of the *Western* members, who objected to the fact that the clause providing for Negroes freed without the means of transportation had been taken out. Still, it is probably fair to suppose that if the slaveholders wanted colonization sufficiently, (and in 1833 $18,000 were appropriated, as stated) they would have gotten it; even if they had to make provision for transportation. There was no unity of opinion on this question among the members of any group of the population and the movement descended into a pleasant diversion, which as Morison suggests, was indulged in, if for any serious purpose, ". . . . in order to

---

186. W. S. Drewry, *The Southampton Insurrection*, Washington, 1900, p. 172 n.
187. "Miscellaneous Papers 1672-1865." *Collections of the Virginia Historical Society, new series*, VI, R. A. Brock ed., Richmond, 1887, p. 30; cited by W. S. Drewry, *op. cit.*, 171.
188. E. L. Fox, *op. cit.*, p. 102.
189. *Ibid.*, p. 94.

protect, and not abolish slavery." Morison also makes the interesting suggestion that the Northern support for the movement to colonize all Negroes came from the fact that it was hoped this might help weaken the political power of the South.[190] But this idea of colonization was not, it appears, seriously held by many people, particularly after Dew demonstrated the extreme difficulty, indeed, impossibility, he thought, of accomplishing it; which argument appeared to John Q. Adams, as to most others, as "conclusive."[191]

Another, and decisive, factor in the decline of the colonization movement was the apparently almost unanimous opposition of the Negroes, who naturally loathed leaving their homes and felt moreover,[192] "America is more our country, than it is the whites—we have enriched it with our *blood and tears.*" It is to be observed that the collapse here mentioned, which was permanent, refers to the movement for the colonization of free Negroes, not of the freed Negroes[193] which was to develop later and still lives, though feebly.[194]

F: HERITAGE

The Turner Revolt also has had some influence as a tradition. Drewry gives evidence of this from the years immediately after the event to the time at which he was writing.[195] The time of the appearance of Higginson's article, August, 1861, is, itself, evidence of the influence of the revolt as a tradition of struggle. Higginson, indeed, said ". . . . its

190. S. E. Morison, *op. cit.,* p. 266, note 12; 267 note 14.
191. *Memoirs of John Quincy Adams* . . . . edited by C. F. Adams, IX, October 13, 1833, p. 23, Philadelphia, 1876.
192. (David) *Walker's appeal, in four articles* . . . . 3rd edition, Boston, 1830, p. 73 (emphasis in original); the sentiments of the Negro Convention in Philadelphia, 1831, as noted previously; E. A. Andrews, letter of July 17, 1835 in *Slavery and the domestic slave-trade* . . . . Boston, 1836, p. 57.
193. This point is made by L. D. Turner, *Anti-Slavery sentiment in American Literature* . . . . Washington, 1929, p. 105.
194. See, for example, the United Press dispatch "Liberia welcomes American Negroes," New York *World-Telegram,* July 8, 1936.
195. *The Southampton Insurrection, op. cit.,* pp. 110 n. 2; 179 (contradicting, however, p. 161), 180 n. 1.

memory endures still fresh now that thirty added years have[196] brought the more formidable presence of General Butler." The attempt by Turner influenced John Brown. Redpath wrote: "Of colored heroes, Nat Turner and Cinques stood first in his esteem," and quoted Brown as having said, "Nat Turner, with fifty men, held Virginia five weeks. The same number, well organized and armed, can shake the system out of the State."[197] This would indicate that Brown was misinformed about the Turner episode, but what one believes is the important thing in determining one's actions, whether the belief is true or not. According to Williams,[198] writing in 1883, the southern Negro ". . . . women have handed down the tradition to their children, and the 'Prophet Nat' is still marching on."

The preservation of the memory of this episode by many of the Negro people is not difficult to understand. W. E. B. Du Bois has written:[199] "There are ever those about him whispering: 'You are nobody; why strive to be somebody? The odds are overwhelming against you—wealth, tradition, learning and guns. Be reasonable. Accept the dole of charity and the cant of missionaries and sink contentedly to your place as humble servants and helpers of the white world.' " Nat Turner was one who refused to "be reasonable," and it is believed that as the present-day stirrings of the American Negro people grow, the significance of the Turner Revolt as a tradition of progressive struggle will increase.

---

196. T. W. Higginson, *Atlantic Monthly*, VIII, 173.
197. J. Redpath, *The public life of John Brown* . . . . London, Boston, 1860, pp. 38, 145.
198. G. W. Williams, *History of the Negro Race* . . . . New York, 1883, II, 91.
199. In *John Brown*, (American Crisis biographies, edited by E. P. Oberholtzer) Philadelphia, 1909, p. 390. Note also the fact that Turner's "Confessions" was reprinted in 1881 in Petersburg, Va.; it had been reprinted earlier, as the bibliography indicates, in E. S. Abdy's *Journal of a Residence* . . . . (1835); it served, too, in part, as the inspiration for Harriet Beecher Stowe's novel, *Dred, A Tale of the Great Dismal Swamp* (1856).

CONCLUSION

W. S. Drewry has two estimates of the Turner Revolt. On one page[1] the reader is told that the revolt ". . . . was, indirectly, most instrumental in bringing about this result (i.e., "the abolition of slavery in the United States"). But, on two other pages[2] he is told: "Servile insurrection tended to delay rather than quicken emancipation."

The latter viewpoint can be correct only if it be true that, prior to the revolt, there was a real desire on the part of the rulers of Virginia to abolish slavery, and that the revolt with the resulting terror and the more vehement anti-slavery propaganda forced them to abandon this desire. If what has here been said is true, this idea is fallacious.

Having, however, refuted the latter does not prove the former, and the former cannot be *proven*. This does appear to be true: The Turner Revolt may be summed up by the one word accelerator. It may itself be considered but an acceleration of the agitation among the slaves of this hemisphere during the five or six years prior to 1831. And the trends observable in those years received an impetus from that event; colonization, repressive legislation, pro-slavery ideological development, abolitionist agitation, all had begun to grow in the years just preceding the revolt and that event accelerated that growth. And other movements, of longer duration, as anti-Negro apprenticeship agitation and sectionalism within Virginia, also became increasingly prominent in the half-decade preceding 1831, and received very considerable impetus from Nat Turner.

---

1. *The Southampton Insurrection*, Washington, 1900, p. 181.
2. *Ibid.*, pp. 186, 193.

Because of these facts it is believed that it may certainly be said the revolt did not retard the abolition of slavery, and that, quite possibly, it hastened that action. Certainly, if one is to understand the genesis of the generation of crisis preceding emancipation he cannot afford to overlook the most important single overt precipitate of that critical period, the Turner Revolt.

Mr. Thomas Nelson Page, to whom Nat Turner was but a "notorious negro,"[3] as all these "inferior" beings[4] are who do not "keep their place" wrote,[5] concerning a white rebellious Nat, one Nathaniel Bacon: ". . . . there are 'rebellions' which are not rebellions, but great revolutions, and there are 'rebels' who, however absolutely their immediate purpose may have failed, and however unjustly contemporary history may have recorded their actions, shall yet be known to posterity as patriots pure and lofty, whose motives and deeds shall evoke the admiration of all succeeding times."

If and when humanism arrives and animalism is driven from the world, Nat Turner will be labeled as one who fought against the latter. His motives will be admired and sadness, and amazement, perhaps, will grip the observer who will realize that, with those admirable motives, society, as then arranged, made his bloody deeds necessary.

---

3. *The Old South, essays social and political,* New York, 1892, p. 169.
4. *Ibid.,* pp. 314 ff.
5. *Ibid.,* p. 18.

BIBLIOGRAPHY

Not all books given in footnotes are mentioned. Only works directly connected with some phase of the revolt are given.

SOURCE PERIODICALS

The *African Repository,* and colonial journal, Volumes VII, VIII, (1831-1832) published by American Colonization Society, Washington, 1832.

The *American Annual Register,* for the year 1830-1831, Boston, (C. Bowen), New York, (E. and G. W. Blunt), 1832.

The *American Annual Register,* for the year 1831-1832, second edition, E. and G. W. Blunt, New York, 1835.

The *Atlas,* Volumes III, IV, 1831 and 1832, New York.

The *Constitutional Whig,* (Richmond), 1831 and 1832.

The *Farmers' Register,* Vol. I, (pp. 5, 36-48) Shellbank, Virginia, 1834.

The *Free Enquirer,* Volume III, 1831, New York.

The *Liberator,* 1831 and 1832, Boston.

The *National Intelligencer,* Washington, 1831.

New York *Evening Post,* 1831.

Niles' Weekly Register, Volumes 36-38; 40-43 (1829-32) Baltimore.

Quarterly Anti-Slavery Magazine, Vol. I, No. 3, (April, 1836) New York.

The *Richmond Enquirer,* 1831 and 1832.

The *Southern Advocate,* (Huntsville, Alabama) 1831.

SOURCE BOOKS AND PAMPHLETS

ABDY, E. S., *Journal of a residence and tour in the United States from April, 1833 to October, 1834,* 3 Volumes, London, 1835, John Murray. This is particularly valuable because in an appendix to the last volume is printed *The Confessions of Nat*

Turner, copied from the now very scarce pamphlet by **Thomas** Gray. The punctuation and capitalization of the original have been changed and misspelling corrected. The lists of Negroes arrested and whites killed, given by Gray, are not reprinted here.

ADAMS, CHARLES FRANCIS, (editor) *Memoirs of John Quincy Adams comprising portions of his diary from 1795 to 1848,* 12 Volumes, Philadelphia, 1874-1877, Vols. VIII, IX, J. P. Lippincott.

ALEXANDER, G. W., *Letters on the slave-trade, slavery, and emancipation; with a reply to objections made to the liberation of slaves in the Spanish Colonies;* addressed to the friends on the continent of Europe, during a visit to Spain and Portugal, London, 1842, Charles Gilpin. This is of value for its notice of the development of British abolitionism in 1830.

(AMES, J. R.) *"Liberty" the image and superscription on every coin issued by the United States of America.* Proclaim liberty throughout all the land unto all the inhabitants thereof—the inscription on the bell in the old Philadelphia statehouse, which was rung July 4, 1776, at the signing of the Declaration of Independence. 1837, (n.p) Valuable for its account of anti-slavery agitation in England, and early denial of innate inferiority hypothesis concerning Negro.

ANDREWS, E. A., *Slavery and the domestic slave-trade in the United States* in a series of letters addressed to the executive committee of the American union for the relief and improvement of the colored race, Boston, 1836, Light and Stearns—a very valuable and straight-forward work.

BALDWIN, T., and J. THOMAS, *A new and complete gazetteer of the United States;* giving a full and comprehensive review of the present condition, industry and resources of the American confederacy; Philadelphia, 1854. On p. 1087 are facts concerning Southampton County.

CHILD, (LYDIA M.) MRS., *An appeal in favor of that class of Americans called Africans,* Boston, 1833, Allen and Ticknor. *Documents containing statistics of Virginia ordered to be printed by the state convention sitting in the city of Richmond,* 1850-51, Richmond, 1851, William Culley.

112

BIBLIOGRAPHY

ELLIOT, E. N., (editor) *Cotton is king, and pro-slavery arguments*: comprising the writings of (J.H.) Hammond, (W.) Harper, (D.) Christy, (T.) Stringfellow, (C.) Hodge, (A.T.) Bledsoe, and (S.A.) Cartwright, on this important subject by E. N. Elliot president of Planters' College, Mississippi, with an essay on slavery in the light of international law by the editor, Augusta, Ga., 1860, Pritchard, Abbott, and Loomis. The article by David Christy is important.

GRAY, THOMAS R., *The Confessions of Nat Turner, the leader* of the late insurrection in Southampton, Va. As fully and voluntarily made to Thomas R. Gray, in the prison where he was confined and acknowledged by him to be such when read before the court of Southampton; with the certificate, under seal of the court convened at Jerusalem, Nov. 5, 1831, for his trial. Also an authentic account of the whole insurrection, with lists of the whites who were murdered, and of the Negroes brought before the court of Southampton, and there sentenced, etc. Baltimore: published by Thomas R. Gray. Lucas & Deaver, print. 1831.

This is the main source for any work on the Turner Revolt. Thousands of copies, it appears, were issued (see The *Liberator,* Vol. I, p. 202, Dec. 17, 1831; The *Southern Advocate,* December 3, 1831; T. W. Higginson, *Travellers and Outlaws,* Boston, 1889, p. 330) but it is now exceedingly scarce. However, it is not so scarce as J. W. Cromwell (*Journal of Negro History,* V, 217 note 17) and B. Brawley (*A Social History of the American Negro. . . .* N.Y., 1921, p. 406) make it, for they say it is not even in the Virginia State Library. It is, and it is also in the 135th Street branch of the New York Public Library. According to Cromwell (*op. cit.*) the Richmond *Enquirer* (he gives no date, the item was not found by the present writer) doubted that Turner used such "classically expressed" language, but no doubts were cast upon the contents of the pamphlet. W. S. Drewry (*The Southampton Insurrection,* Washington, 1900, p. 169 n.) states that it could not be sold in the South. As far as the present writer knows, it is genuine.

HAMILTON, J. G. de ROULHAC, edited and collected *The papers of Thomas Ruffin,* publication of the North Carolina Historical Commission, Raleigh, 1918, 2 Vols. Edward and Broughton. In volume two there are very valuable contemporary letters on the revolt.

Journal of the house of delegates of the Commonwealth of Virginia, begun and held at the Capitol, in the city of Richmond, on Monday, the fifth of December, one thousand eight hundred and thirty one. Richmond, 1831, Thomas Ritchie.

Laws of the state of Delaware from the sixteenth day of January, one thousand eight hundred and thirty, to the thirteenth day of February, one thousand eight hundred and thirty-five to which is prefixed the amended Constitution of said state, Volume VIII, Dover, 1841, S. Kimmey.

Acts of the legislative council of the *Territory of Florida* passed at the tenth sessions, commencing January 2d, and ending February 12, 1832, Tullahasse, 1832, William Wilson.

Acts of the General assembly of the *State of Georgia* passed in Millidgeville at an annual session in November and December, 1831, Millidgeville, 1832, Prince and Ragland.

Acts passed at the first session of the forty-first general assembly for the *commonwealth of Kentucky*, begun and held in the town of Frankfort on Monday, 3rd day of December in the year 1832, and of the commonwealth the forty-first, John Breathitt, Governor. Frankfort, 1833. A. G. Hodges.

Acts passed at the first session of the ninth legislature of the *state of Louisiana* begun and held in the city of New Orleans on Monday, the 8th day of December in the year of our Lord 1828, of the independence of the United States of America the fifty-second, New Orleans, 1829, John Gibson.

Acts passed at the extra session of the tenth legislature *of the state of Louisiana* begun and held in the city of New Orleans on Monday, the 14th day of November 1831, New Orleans, 1831, John Gibson.

Laws made and passed by the general assembly of the *state of Maryland* in Annapolis, begun Monday the 26th day of December, ended on Wednesday the 14th day of March 1832. Annapolis, 1832, J. Hughes.

Laws of the *state of Mississippi* passed at the 14th session of the general assembly held in the town of Jackson, Jackson, 1830, Peter Isler.

114

A digest of the *laws of Mississippi* comprising all the laws of a general nature, including the acts of the session of 1839, by T. J. Fox Alden and J. A. Van Hoesen, New York, 1839, A. S. Gould.

Acts passed by the general assembly of the *state of North Carolina* at the session of 1831-32, Raleigh 1832, Lawrence and Lemay.

Acts of the general assembly of the *state of North Carolina* at the session of 1828-29, Raleigh, 1829, Lawrence and Lemay.

Acts and resolutions of the general assembly of the *state of South Carolina* passed in December 1831, Columbia 1832, A. Landrum.

Public acts passed at the stated session of the nineteenth general assembly of *the state of Tennessee* 1831, Nashville, 1832, A. A. Hall, F. S. Heiskell.

Acts passed at a general assembly of the *commonwealth of Virginia* begun and held at the capitol in the city of Richmond on Monday, the sixth day of December in the year of our Lord, one thousand eight hundred and thirty, and of the Commonwealth the fifty-fifth. To which are prefixed the declaration of rights and the constitution of Virginia, Richmond, 1831, Thomas Ritchie.

Acts passed at a general assembly of the *commonwealth of Virginia* begun and held at the capitol in the city of Richmond on Monday, the fifth day of December in the year of our Lord, 1831, and of the Commonwealth the 56th, Richmond, 1832, Thomas Ritchie.

MARTINEAU, HARRIET. *Society in America*, fourth edition, 2 Volumes, New York, London, 1837, Saunder and Otley.

OLCOTT, CHARLES; *Two lectures on the subject of slavery and abolition* compiled for the special use of anti-slavery lecturers and debaters and intended for public reading, Massillon, Ohio, 1838, printed for author. Interesting for its vigorous denunciation of innate inferiority idea; and suggests compensation of the liberated slaves, not their former masters.

Proceedings and debates of the Virginia state convention of 1829-1830 to which are subjoined the new constitution of Virginia and the votes of the people. Richmond, 1830, printed by Samuel Shepherd for Ritchie and Cook.

The Pro-slavery argument: as maintained by the most distinguished writers of the southern states: containing the several essays on the subject of Chancellor (William) Harper, Governor

(J.H.) Hammond, Dr. (W. G.) Simms, and Professor (T.R.) Dew. Charleston, 1852.

SUNDERLAND, REV. LA ROY; *Anti-Slavery manual,* containing a collection of facts and arguments on American slavery, New York, 1837, second edition.

Virginia slavery debate of 1832 (bound volume of pamphlets in Virginia State Library, printed by T. W. White, 1832, Richmond) containing the letters of Appomattox (B. W. Leigh) to the people of Virginia; and the speeches of Henry Berry of Jefferson, Jan. 20; P. A. Bolling of Buckingham, Jan. 11; W. H. Brodnax of Dinwiddie, Jan. 19; J. T. Brown of Petersburg, Jan. 18; J. A. Chandler of Norfolk County, Jan. 17; C. J. Faulkner of Berkeley, Jan. 20; James McDowell, Jr., of Rockbridge, Jan. 21; Thomas Marshall of Fanquier, Jan. 14; T. J. Randolph of Albermarle, Jan. 21; and an appendix by W. H. Brodnax explaining his colonization bill.

Walker's (David) *Appeal,* in four articles together with a preamble to the coloured citizens of the world, but in particular, and very expressly to those of the United States of America, written in Boston, state of Massachusetts, September 28, 1829. Third and last edition with additional notes, corrections, etc. Boston, revised and published by David Walker, 1830.

WARNER (SAMUEL), *Authentic and impartial narrative of the tragical scene which was witnessed in Southampton County,* (Virginia) on Monday the 22d of August last, when fifty-five of its inhabitants (mostly women and children) were inhumanly massacred by the blacks! Communicated by those who were eye witnesses of the bloody scene, and confirmed by the confessions of several of the Blacks while under sentence of death. Printed for Warner and West 1831 (registered in New York, October 21, 1831 by Samuel Warner as author). This pamphlet is almost wholly inaccurate but rumors are often quite as important as facts.

SECONDARY PERIODICALS

BALLAGH, JAMES CURTIS; The anti-slavery sentiment in Virginia, *South Atlantic Quarterly,* April, 1902, Vol. I, No. 2, pp. 107-117.

CROMWELL, JOHN W.; The aftermath of Nat Turner's Insurrection, *Journal of Negro History*, April, 1920, Vol. V, no. 2, pp. 208-234.

HIGGINSON, THOMAS W.; Nat Turner's Insurrection, *Atlantic Monthly*, August, 1861, Vol. VIII, pp. 173-187.

JACKSON, LUTHER, P.; Religious instruction of Negroes, 1830-1860, with special reference to South Carolina, *Journal of Negro History*, Volume XV, 1930, pp. 72-114.

JOHNSTON, JAMES H.; The participation of white men in Virginia Negro insurrections, *Journal of Negro History*, XVI, 1931, pp. 158-167.

LAWSON, ELIZABETH; After Nat Turner's revolt, *Daily Worker*, New York, August 21, 1936.

PARKER, WILLIAM H.; The Nat Turner insurrection, *Old Virginia Yarns*, Vol. I, No. 1, January, 1893, pp. 14-29. There is no title page—the preceding is written in pencil. The copy is in the Virginia State Library.

RAPPOPORT, STANLEY; Slave struggles for freedom, *The Crisis*, September, 1936, pp. 264, 265, 274, 284-286.

STEVENS, N.; The 100th anniversary of the Nat Turner revolt. *The Communist*, August, 1931, Vol. X, No. 8, pp. 737-743.

WEEKS, STEPHEN B.; The slave insurrection in Virginia, 1831 known as 'Old Nat's War', *Magazine of American History*, June, 1891, Vol. XXV, pp. 448-458.

Virginia Magazine of History and Biography, Vol. VIII, June 1901, pp. 221-222, a review of W. S. Drewry's *The Southampton Insurrection*, Washington, 1900.

Virginia Magazine of History and Biography, published quarterly by the Virginia Historical Society, Vol. XI, 1904, "Genealogy of Bruce family," p. 331.

Virginia Magazine of History and Biography, Vol. XXXVI, 1928, "Genealogy of Harrison of James River," p. 277 n.

William and Mary College Quarterly Historical Magazine, Vol. XXIV, 1915, (first series) "Genealogy of the Lee family," p. 52.

SECONDARY BOOKS

ADAMS, ALICE DANA; *The neglected period of anti-slavery agitation in America, 1808-1831*. Radcliffe College Monograph No. 14, Boston and London, 1908.

AMBLER, CHARLES HENRY; *Sectionalism in Virginia from 1776 to 1861*, Chicago, 1910, University of Chicago press.

AMBLER, C. H.; *Thomas Ritchie, a study in Virginia politics*, Richmond, 1913, Bell Book and Stationery Company.

BALLAGH, JAMES CURTIS; *A History of slavery in Virginia*, Baltimore, 1902, Johns Hopkins University studies in historical and political science, extra volume XXIV.

BARBER, J. W.; *Incidents in American history*, pp. 262-268. New York, 1847, C. F. Cooledge and Bro.

BARNES, GILBERT H.; *The anti-slavery impulse 1830-1844*, The American Historical Association, New York, London, 1933, D. Appleton—Century.

BASSETT, John Spencer; *Slavery in the state of North Carolina*. Baltimore, 1899, Introduction and Chapters IV, V; Johns Hopkins University studies in historical and political science, series XVII, 7-8.

BELL, LANDON C.; *The Old Free State*, a contribution to the history of Lunenburg County and southside Virginia, Richmond, 1927, 2 volumes, William Byrd Press, esp. Chapter XI, Vol. I.

BEMIS, SAMUEL FLAGG; (editor) *The American secretaries of state and their diplomacy*, essay on Henry Clay by Theodore Burton, Vol. IV, New York, 1928, A. A. Knopf.

BRACKETT, JEFFREY R.; *The Negro in Maryland*, a study of the institution of slavery, Baltimore, 1889, Johns Hopkins University studies in historical and political science, extra volume VI.

BRAWLEY, BENJAMIN; *A social history of the American Negro*, being a history of the Negro problem in the United States including a history and study of the republic of Liberia, esp. 132-154, New York, 1921, Macmillan.

BROCK, R. A.; "Miscellaneous papers 1672-1865 now first printed from the manuscripts in the collections of the Virginia Historical Society," *Collections of the Virginia historical society*, new series, Vol. VI, Richmond, 1887, pp. 23-31.

BRUCE, WILLIAM CABELL, *Below the James*, a plantation sketch, New York, 1918, Neale, pp. 152-153.

BRYANT, WILLIAM CULLEN, and S. H. GRAY, *A popular his-*

tory of the United States, four volumes, New York, 1881, IV, 319-322, C. Scribner.

(BUCHANAN, JAMES); *Mr. Buchanan's administration on the eve of the rebellion,* Chapter I, New York, 1866, D. Appleton. Published also in Vol. XII of John B. Moore's *The Works of James Buchanan,* Philadelphia and New York, 1911, J. P. Lippincott.

BURGESS, JOHN W.; *The Middle period 1817-1858,* (the American history series) New York, 1898, Scribner's sons, Chapter XI.

CHANDLER, JULIAN, A. C.; *Representation in Virginia,* Baltimore, 1896, Johns Hopkins University studies in historical and political science, series 14, 6-7, esp. pp. 32-44.

CHANNING, EDWARD; *A history of the United States,* six volumes, Vol. V, the period of transition, pages 120-171, New York, 1931, Macmillan.

COBB, THOMAS R. R.; *An inquiry into the law of Negro slavery in the United States* to which is prefixed a historical sketch of slavery, Philadelphia, 1858, T. and J. W. Johnson; Savannah, W. T. Williams.

CURTIS, G. T.; *Life of James Buchanan, fifteenth president of the United States,* 2 Vols. N. Y. London, 1883, II, 202-286. Harper and Bros.

COFFIN, JOSHUA; *An account of some of the principal slave insurrections, and others, which have occurred, or been attempted, in the United States* and elsewhere, during the last two centuries with various remarks, New York, 1860, published by the American Anti-Slavery Society. This is a rather poor work, but there are so few in this field that its value is enhanced.

COOKE, JOHN E.; *Virginia, a history of her people,* (American Commonwealths, edited by H. E. Scudder) Boston, 1883, pp. 485-487, Houghton, Mifflin.

COUPLAND, R.; *The British Anti-Slavery Movement,* London, 1933, Home University library, pp. 112-150. Butterworth.

CRAVEN, AVERY O.; *Soil exhaustion as a factor in the agricultural history of Virginia and Maryland 1806-1860,* Urbana, 1926, University of Illinois studies in social sciences, XIII, No. 1.

CRAVEN, A. O.; *Edmund Ruffin southerner, a study of secession.* New York and London, 1932, esp. pp. 107-142, D. Appleton.

CROMWELL, JOHN W.; *The Negro in American history,* men and women eminent in the evolution of the American of African descent, Washington, 1914, Chapters IV, XI, American Negro Academy.

CUTLER, JAMES ELBERT; *Lynch-law, an investigation into the history of lynching in the United States,* New York, London, Bombay, 1905, Longmans, Green. pp. 92-96.

DODD, WILLIAM E.; *The cotton kingdom, a chronicle of the old South,* (Vol. 27, Chronicles of America, A. Johnson, editor). Yale University Press, New Haven, 1919.

DREWRY, WILLIAM SIDNEY; *The Southampton Insurrection,* Washington, 1900, Neale; also published as *Slave Insurrections in Virginia,* same place and date. The book is valuable for the rumors and reminiscences it presents. It is notable for exceedingly poor documentation and often very uncritical and contradictory statements. The pictures are the best part of the book.

DU BOIS, W. E. BURGHARDT; *John Brown,* (American Crisis biographies, edited by E. P. Oberholtzer) Philadelphia, 1909.

Encyclopaedia Britannica, 14th edition, (1929) Vol. 22, p. 628.

Federal Aid in domestic disturbances 1787-1903, prepared under the direction of Maj.-Gen. Henry C. Corbin by Frederick T. Wilson, Senate document number 209, 57th Cong. 2d session, (Vol. 15) pp. 56, 261-264, Government Printing Office, Washington, 1903.

FOX, E. L.; *The American Colonization Society 1817-1840,* Johns Hopkins Un. studies, Baltimore, 1919, XXXVII, no. 3.

GARLAND, HUGH A.; *The Life of John Randolph of Roanoke,* (2 vols.) complete in one volume, eleventh edition, New York, 1857, D. Appleton, pp. 324 ff.

(GARRISON, W. P. and F. J.); *William Lloyd Garrison 1805-1879,* the story of his life told by his children, 2 Vols. New York, 1885, Vol. I, pp. 219-276. The Century Co.

GOODLOE, DANIEL R.; *The Southern Platform*: or manual of southern sentiment on the subject of slavery, Boston, 1858, J. P. Jewett.

GRAY, LEWIS CECIL, (assisted by E. K. Thompson); *History of Agriculture in the southern United States* to 1860, 2 Vols. Washington, 1933. Carnegie Institution.

GRIMKE, ARCHIBALD H.; *William Lloyd Garrison, the abolitionist*, New York, London, Toronto, 1891, pp. 118-132, Funk and Wagnalls.

Harper's Encyclopaedia of United States. London, 1902, IX, 133-134.

HART, ALBERT BUSHNELL; *Slavery and Abolition 1831-1841*, (Vol. 16 of the American Nation: A history, edited by A. B. Hart) Chapters 15 and 16, New York and London, 1906, Harper and Brothers.

HENRY, H. M.; *The police control of the slave in South Carolina*, Emory, Virginia, 1914 (doctoral dissertation, Vanderbilt University) 153 ff.

HERBERT, HILARY A.; *The abolition crusade and its consequences—four periods of American History*, New York, 1912, C. Scribner's Sons.

HIGGINSON, THOMAS WENTWORTH; *Travellers and Outlaws, episodes in American History* with an appendix of authorities, pp. 276-330, Boston (Lee & Shepard), New York (C. T. Dillingham), 1889. There are some errors in this, but considering the limited space, it is an excellent treatment. One pamphlet of twelve pages by Henry Bibb mentioned here has not been found.

HINTON, J. H. and S. L. KNAPP and J. O. CHOULES; *The History and topography of the United States of North America*, second edition, 2 vols., Boston, 1846, Vol. II, S. Walker.

HOLST, H. von; *The Constitutional and political history of the United States* translated by J. J. Lalor, 7 Vols. 1877-1892, Vol. II, 1828-1846, Chicago, 1879, Callaghan and Co.

HOWISON, ROBERT R.; *A History of Virginia from its discovery and settlement by Europeans to the present time*, 2 Vols., Vol. II, 1763-1847, pp. 439-446; 498-500, Richmond (Drinkes and Morris) New York and London (Wiley and Putnam) 1848.

JAMES BARTLETT, B.; (edits and continues) *History of Maryland* by James McSherry, Baltimore, 1904, Baltimore Book Co.

JAMES, G. P. R.; *The Old Dominion, a novel*, London and New

York, 1858, a new edition, G. Routledge, (Virginia State Library). This is a love story with the revolt as a background.

JAMES, MARQUIS, *The Raven, a biography of Sam Houston,* pp. 181 ff., 374, New York, 1929, Blue Ribbon.

JENKINS, WILLIAM SUMMER; *Pro-slavery thought in the old South,* University of North Carolina press, Chapel Hill, 1935. This is painstaking but logography, not history.

LUNDY, BENJAMIN, *The Life, Travels and Opinions of*—including his journeys to Texas and Mexico; with a sketch of contemporary events, and a notice of the revolution in Hayti compiled under the direction and on behalf of his children, Philadelphia, 1847, Merrihew and Thompson. According to the *Encyclopaedia Britannica* this was written by Thomas Earle (14th ed., Vol. 14, p. 485). Where this information was obtained is not known. The book was registered by William D. Parrish.

MACY, JESSE; *The anti-slavery crusade, a chronicle of the gathering storm* (Chronicles of America, Vol. 28, edited by A. Johnson) Yale University Press, New Haven, 1921, esp. pp. 54-66.

McMASTER, JOHN BACH; *A History of the People of the United States, from the revolution to the Civil War,* 7 Vols., Vol. VI, 1830-1842, New York, 1906, pp. 69-113. D. Appleton.

McSHERRY, JAMES; *History of Maryland from its first settlement in 1634 to the year 1848,* second edition, revised and corrected by the author, Baltimore, 1849, esp. p. 358. John Murphy.

MOORE, JOHN W.; *History of North Carolina from its earliest discoveries to the present time,* 2 Vols. Raleigh, 1880, Vol. II, esp. pp. 30-31.

MORISON, SAMUEL E.; *The Life and Letters of Harrison Gray Otis, Federalist 1765-1848,* 2 Vols. Boston and New York, 1913, Vol. II, pp. 256-283, Houghton Mifflin. The letters here are very valuable.

MUNFORD, BEVERLEY, B.; *Virginia's attitude toward slavery and secession,* Chapters 8 and 9, New York, London, Bombay, Calcutta, 1909. Longmans, Green.

The *National Cyclopaedia of American Biography,* Vol. XIII, 597, New York, J. T. White.

OLMSTED, FREDERICK L.; *A Journey in the seaboard slave states in the years 1853-1854* with remarks on their economy (originally issued in 1856) with a biographical sketch by F. L. Olmsted, Jr., and an introduction by W. P. Trent. 2 Vols. New York and London, 1904, Vol. I, G. P. Putnam's Sons.

OLMSTED, F. L.; *A Journey in the back country,* London, 1860, pp. 158-204, Sampson Low.

PAGE, THOMAS NELSON, *The Old South,* essays, social and political, New York, 1892, C. Scribner's Sons.

PAULDING, JAMES E.; *Slavery in the United States,* New York, 1836, Harper.

PHILLIPS, ULRICH B.; *Racial problems, adjustments and disturbances* in the antebellum south, reprinted from *The South in the Building of the nation,* Vol. IV, 194-241. Richmond, 1909, Southern Publican Society.

PHILLIPS, U. B.; *American Negro Slavery,* a survey of the supply, employment and control of Negro Labor as determined by the plantation regime, New York, London, 1918. D. Appleton.

PHILLIPS, U. B.; *Life and labor in the old South,* Students' edition, Boston, 1929, Little, Brown.

REDPATH, JAMES; *The public life of Captain John Brown,* with an autobiography of his childhood and youth. London (Thickbroom and Stapleton), Boston, (Thayer & Eldridge) 1860, pp. 38, 145.

RHODES, JAMES FORD; *History of the United States from the compromise of 1850,* Vol. I, 1850-1854, New York, 1896, pp. 1-98; 303-383, Harper.

SANBORN, F. B.; *The Life and letters of John Brown, Liberator of Kansas, and martyr of Virginia,* Boston, 1891, Roberts, p. 34.

SCHOULER, JAMES; *History of the United States of America under the constitution,* 6 Vols, 1894-1899, revised, Vol. IV, 1831-1847, pp. 206-238, New York, 1894, Dodd, Mead.

SCHURZ, CARL; *Life of Henry Clay* (American statesmen, edited by J. R. Morse, Jr.) 2 Vols, Vol. II, Chapter XVII, Boston and New York, 1890, Houghton, Mifflin.

SHANKS, H. T.; *The secession movement in Virginia, 1847-1861*, p. 1-17, Richmond, 1934, Garrett and Massie.

SIMMS, HENRY H.; *The Rise of the Whigs in Virginia, 1824-1840*, (doctoral dissertation, Columbia) Richmond, 1929, Wm. Byrd, esp. pp. 36-39.

STEVENSON, RICHARD T.; *The Growth of the Nation, 1809-1837*, being volume XII of the History of North America, 20 Vols. edited by G. C. Lee, Philadelphia, 1905, pp. 305-344, Lippincott.

STROUD, GEORGE M.; *A Sketch of the laws relating to slavery in the several states of the United States of America*, second edition, Philadelphia, 1856, Henry Longstreth.

STRYKER, LLOYD P.; *Andrew Johnson, a study in courage*, New York, 1929, pp. 36-51, Macmillan.

SWEM, E. G.; *Virginia Historical index*, Roanoke, Virginia, 1934-1936, Stone Printing Company. A valuable aid in research.

TURNER, LORENZO, D.; *Anti-slavery sentiment in American Literature prior to 1865*, Washington, 1929, The Association for the study of Negro life and history.

WAGSTAFF, H. M.; *State rights and political parties in North Carolina 1776-1861*, Baltimore 1906, Johns Hopkins Un. Studies in historical and political science, XXIV, Nos. 7-8, esp. pp. 56-58.

WATERMAN, WILLIAM R.; *Frances Wright*, Columbia University studies in history, economics and public law, Vol. CXV, No. 1, Chapters II, III, New York, 1924.

WEATHERFORD, W. D., JOHNSON, C. S.; *Race Relations*: Adjustment of whites and Negroes in the United States, New York, 1934, pp. 260-273, D. C. Heath.

WESTON, GEORGE M.; *The progress of slavery in the United States*, Washington, 1857. Even to the brevity of its title this would be a good twentieth century book.

WHITFIELD, THEODORE M.; *Slavery agitation in Virginia 1829-1832*, Baltimore, 1930, Johns Hopkins University studies in historical and political science, extra volumes, new series, No. 10.

WILSON, HENRY; *History of the rise and fall of the slave power in America*, 2 Vols. Boston, 1872, Vol. I, pp. 165-207. James R. Osgood.

BIBLIOGRAPHY

WILSON, HILL P.; *John Brown, soldier of fortune, a critique*, Lawrence, Kansas, 1913, published by author, pp. 357, 360-362.

WISE, BARTON H.; *The life of Henry A. Wise of Virginia 1806-1876*, Chap. 4, New York and London, 1899, Macmillan.

WOODSON, CARTER G.; *The education of the Negro prior to 1861*, a history of the education of the colored people of the United States from the beginning of slavery to the Civil War, New York and London, 1915, pp. 162-164, C. P. Putnam's Sons.

WOODSON, C. G.; *The Negro in our history*, fifth edition, Washington, 1928, The Associated publishers, pp. 180-187.

THE
CONFESSIONS
OF
NAT TURNER,

THE LEADER OF THE LATE

INSURRECTION IN SOUTHAMPTON, VA.

As fully and voluntarily made to

THOMAS R. GRAY,

In the prison where he was confined, and acknowledged by
him to be such when read before the Court of Southampton; with the certificate, under seal of
the Court convened at Jerusalem,
Nov. 5, 1831, for his trial.

ALSO, AN AUTHENTIC

ACCOUNT OF THE WHOLE INSURRECTION,

WITH LISTS OF THE WHITES WHO WERE MURDERED,

AND OF THE NEGROES BROUGHT BEFORE THE COURT OF
SOUTHAMPTON, AND THERE SENTENCED, &c.

Baltimore:
PUBLISHED BY THOMAS R. GRAY.
Lucas & Deaver, print.
1831.

Original title page photographed.

APPENDIX

THE
CONFESSIONS
of
NAT TURNER,
The Leader of the Late
INSURRECTION IN SOUTHAMPTON, VA.

As fully and voluntarily made to
THOMAS R. GRAY,

In the prison where he was confined, and acknowledged by
him to be such when read before the Court of Southampton; with the certificate, under seal of
the Court, convened at Jerusalem,
Nov. 5, 1831, for his trial.

Also, An Authentic

ACCOUNT OF THE WHOLE INSURRECTION.

With Lists Of The Whites Who Were Murdered.

And Of The Negroes Brought Before The Court Of
Southampton, And There Sentenced, &.

Baltimore:

PUBLISHED BY THOMAS R. GRAY.
Lucas & Deaver, print.
1831.

127

DISTRICT OF COLUMBIA, TO WIT:

Be it remembered, That on this tenth day of November, Anno Domini, eighteen hundred and thirty-one, Thomas R. Gray of the said District, deposited in this office the title of a book, which is in the words as following:

"The Confessions of Nat Turner, the leader of the late insurrection in Southampton, Virginia, as fully and voluntarily made to Thomas R. Gray, in the prison where he was confined, and acknowledged by him to be such when read before the Court of Southampton; with the certificate, under seal, of the Court convened at Jerusalem, November 5, 1831, for his trial. Also, an authentic account of the whole insurrection, with lists of the whites who were murdered, and of the negroes brought before the Court of Southampton, and there sentenced, &. the right whereof he claims as proprietor, in conformity with an Act of Congress, entitled "An act to amend the several acts respecting Copy Rights."

(Seal.)

EDMUND J. LEE, Clerk of the District.
In testimony that the above is a true copy, from the record of the District Court for the District of Columbia, I, Edmund J. Lee, the Clerk thereof, have hereunto set my hand and affixed the seal of my office, this 10th day of November, 1831.
EDMUND J. LEE, C. D. C.

TO THE PUBLIC.

The late insurrection in Southampton has greatly excited the public mind, and led to a thousand idle, exaggerated and mischievous reports. It is the first instance in our history of an open rebellion of the slaves, and attended with such

atrocious circumstances of cruelty and destruction, as could
not fail to leave a deep impression, not only upon the minds
of the community where this fearful tragedy was wrought,
but throughout every portion of our country, in which this
population is to be found. Public curiosity has been on the
stretch to understand the origin and progress of this dreadful
conspiracy, and the motives which influence its diabolical
actors. The insurgent slaves had all been destroyed, or apprehended, tried and executed, (with the exception of the
leader,) without revealing any thing at all satisfactory, as
to the motives which governed them, or the means by which
they expected to accomplish their object. Every thing connected with the sad affair was wrapt in mystery, until Nat
Turner, the leader of this ferocious band, whose name has
resounded throughout our widely extended empire, was
captured. This "great Bandit" was taken by a single individual, in a cave near the residence of his late owner, on
Sunday, the thirtieth of October, without attempting to make
the slightest resistance, and on the following day safely
lodged in the jail of the County. His captor was Benjamin
Phipps, armed with a shot gun well charged. Nat's only
weapon was a small light sword which he immediately sur-
rendered, and begged that his life might be spared. Since
his confinement, by permission of the Jailor, I have had
ready access to him, and finding that he was willing to make
a full and free confession of the origin, progress and con-
summation of the insurrectory movements of the slaves of
which he was the contriver and head; I determined for the
gratification of public curiosity to commit his statements to
writing, and publish them, with little or no variation, from
his own words. That this is a faithful record of his confessions, the annexed certificate of the County Court of Southampton, will attest. They certainly bear one stamp of truth
and sincerity. He makes no attempt (as all the other insurgents who were examined did,) to exculpate himself, but
frankly acknowledges his full participation in all the guilt

of the transaction. He was not only the contriver of the conspiracy, but gave the first blow towards its execution.

It will thus appear, that whilst every thing upon the surface of society wore a calm and peaceful aspect; whilst not one note of preparation was heard to warn the devoted inhabitants of woe and death, a gloomy fanatic was revolving in the recesses of his own dark, bewildered, and overwrought mind, schemes of indiscriminate massacre to the whites. Schemes too fearfully executed as far as his fiendish band proceeded in their desolating march. No cry for mercy penetrated their flinty bosoms. No acts of remembered kindness made the least impression upon these remorseless murderers. Men, women and children, from hoary age to helpless infancy were involved in the same cruel fate. Never did a band of savages do their work of death more unsparingly. Apprehension for their own personal safety seems to have been the only principle of restraint in the whole course of their bloody proceedings. And it is not the least remarkable feature in this horrid transaction, that a band actuated by such hellish purposes, should have resisted so feebly, when met by the whites in arms. Desperation alone, one would think, might have led to greater efforts. More than twenty of them attacked Dr. Blunt's house on Tuesday morning, a little before day-break, defended by two men and three boys. They fled precipitately at the first fire; and their future plans of mischief, were entirely disconcerted and broken up. Escaping thence, each individual sought his own safety either in concealment, or by returning home, with the hope that his participation might escape detection, and all were shot down in the course of a few days, or captured and brought to trial and punishment. Nat has survived all his followers, and the gallows will speedily close his career. His own account of the conspiracy is submitted to the public, without comment. It reads an awful, and it is hoped, a useful lesson, as to the operations of a mind like his, endeavoring to grapple with things beyond its reach. How it first became

130

bewildered and confounded, and finally corrupted and led to the conception and perpetration of the most atrocious and heart-rending deeds. It is calculated also to demonstrate the policy of our laws in restraint of this class of our population, and to induce all those entrusted with their execution, as well as our citizens generally, to see that they are strictly and rigidly enforced. Each particular community should look to its own safety, whilst the general guardians of the laws, keep a watchful eye over all. If Nat's statements can be relied on, the insurrection in this county was entirely local, and his designs confided but to a few, and these in his immediate vicinity. It was not instigated by motives of revenge or sudden anger, but the results of long deliberation, and a settled purpose of mind. The offspring of gloomy fanaticism, acting upon materials but too well prepared for such impressions. It will be long remembered in the annals of our country, and many a mother as she presses her infant darling to her bosom, will shudder at the recollection of Nat Turner, and his band of ferocious miscreants.

Believing the following narrative, by removing doubts and conjectures from the public mind which otherwise must have remained, would give general satisfaction, it is respectfully submitted to the public by their ob't serv't,

T. R. GRAY.

Jerusalem, Southampton, Va. Nov. 5, 1831.

We the undersigned, members of the Court convened at Jerusalem, on Saturday, the 5th day of Nov. 1831, for the trial of Nat, *alias* Nat Turner, a negro slave, late the property of Putnam Moore, deceased, do hereby certify, that the confessions of Nat, to Thomas R. Gray, was read to him in our presence, and that Nat acknowledged the same to be full, free, and voluntary; and that furthermore, when called upon by the presiding Magistrate of the Court, to state if he had any thing to say, why sentence of death should not be passed upon him, replied he had nothing further than he had communicated to Mr. Gray. Given under our hands and seals at Jerusalem, this 5th day of November, 1831.

JEREMIAH COBB,	[Seal.]
THOMAS PRETLOW,	[Seal.]
JAMES W. PARKER	[Seal.]
CARR BOWERS,	[Seal.]
SAMUEL B. HINES,	[Seal.]
ORRIS A. BROWNE,	[Seal.]

State of Virginia, Southampton County, to wit:

I, James Rochelle, Clerk of the County Court of Southampton in the State of Virginia, do hereby certify, that Jeremiah Cobb, Thomas Pretlow, James W. Parker, Carr Bowers, Samuel B. Hines, and Orris A. Browne, esqr's are acting Justices of the Peace, in and for the County aforesaid, and were members of the Court which convened at Jerusalem, on Saturday the 5th day of November, 1831, for the trial of Nat *alias* Nat Turner, a negro slave, late the property of Putnam Moore, deceased, who was tried and convicted, as an insurgent in the late insurrection in the county of Southampton aforesaid, and that full faith and credit are due, and ought to be given to their acts as Justices of the peace aforesaid.

[Seal.]

In testimony whereof, I have hereunto set my hand and caused the seal of the Court aforesaid, to be affixed this 5th day of November, 1831

JAMES ROCHELLE,

C. S. C. C.

CONFESSION.

Agreeable to his own appointment, on the evening he was committed to prison, with permission of the jailer, I visited NAT on Tuesday the 1st November, when, without being questioned at all, he commenced his narrative in the following words:—

SIR,—You have asked me to give a history of the motives which induced me to undertake the late insurrection, as you call it—To do so I must go back to the days of my infancy, and even before I was born. I was thirty-one years of age the 2nd of October last, and born the property of Benj. Turner, of this county. In my childhood a circumstance occurred which made an indelible impression on my mind, and laid the ground work of that enthusiasm, which has terminated so fatally to many, both white and black, and for which I am about to atone at the gallows. It is here necessary to relate this circumstance—trifling as it may seem, it was the commencement of that belief which has grown with time, and even now, sir, in this dungeon, helpless and forsaken as I am, I cannot divest myself of. Being at play with other children, when three or four years old, I was telling them something, which my mother overhearing, said it had happened before I was born—I stuck to my story, however, and related somethings which went, in her opinion, to confirm it—others being called on were greatly astonished, knowing that these things had happened, and caused them to say in my hearing, I surely would be a prophet, as the Lord had shewn me things that had happened before my birth. And my father and mother strengthened me in this my first impression, saying in my presence, I was intended for some great purpose, which they had always thought from certain marks on my head and breast—[a parcel of excrescences which I believe are not at all uncommon, particularly among negroes, as I have seen several with the same. In this case he has either cut them off or they have nearly disappeared]—My grandmother, who was very religious, and to whom I was much attached—my master, who belonged to the church, and other religious persons who visited the house, and whom I often saw at prayers, noticing

133

the singularity of my manners, I suppose, and my uncommon intelligence for a child, remarked I had too much sense to be raised, and if I was, I would never be of any service to any one as a slave—To a mind like mine, restless, inquisitive and observant of every thing that was passing, it is easy to suppose that religion was the subject to which it would be directed, and although this subject principally occupied my thoughts—there was nothing that I saw or heard of to which my attention was not directed—The manner in which I learned to read and write, not only had great influence on my own mind, as I acquired it with the most perfect ease, so much so, that I have no recollection whatever of learning the alphabet—but to the astonishment of the family, one day, when a book was shewn to me to keep me from crying, I began spelling the names of different objects—this was a source of wonder to all in the neighborhood, particularly the blacks—and this learning was constantly improved at all opportunities—when I got large enough to go to work, while employed, I was reflecting on many things that would present themselves to my imagination, and whenever an opportunity occurred of looking at a book, when the school children were getting their lessons, I would find many things that the fertility of my own imagination had depicted to me before; all my time, not devoted to my master's service, was spent either in prayer, or in making experiments in casting different things in moulds made of earth, in attempting to make paper, gun-powder, and many other experiments, that although I could not perfect, yet convinced me of its practicablity if I had the means.* I was not addicted to stealing in my youth, nor have ever been—Yet such was the confidence of the negroes in the neighborhood, even at this early period of my life, in my superior judgment, that they would often carry me with them when they were going on any roguery, to plan

---

*When questioned as to the manner of manufacturing those different articles, he was found well informed on the subject.

for them. Growing up among them, with this confidence in my superior judgment, and when this, in their opinions, was perfected by Divine inspiration, from the circumstances already alluded to in my infancy, and which belief was ever afterwards zealously inculcated by the austerity of my life and manners, which became the subject of remark by white and black.—Having soon discovered to be great, I must appear so, and therefore studiously avoided mixing in society, and wrapped myself in mystery, devoting my time to fasting and prayer—By this time, having arrived to man's estate, and hearing the scriptures commented on at meetings, I was struck with that particular passage which says: "Seek ye the kingdom of Heaven and all things shall be added unto you." I reflected much on this passage, and prayed daily for light on this subject—As I was praying one day at my plough, the spirit spoke to me, saying "Seek ye the kingdom of Heaven and all things shall be added unto you." *Question*—what do you mean by the Spirit. *Ans.* The Spirit that spoke to the prophets in former days—and I was greatly astonished, and for two years prayed continually, whenever my duty would permit—and then again I had the same revelation, which fully confirmed me in the impression that I was ordained for some great purpose in the hands of the Almighty. Several years rolled round, in which many events occurred to strengthen me in this my belief. At this time I reverted in my mind to the remarks made of me in my childhood, and the things that had been shewn me—and as it had been said of me in my childhood by those by whom I had been taught to pray, both white and black, and in whom I had the greatest confidence, that I had too much sense to be raised, and if I was, I would never be of any use to any one as a slave. Now finding I had arrived to man's estate, and was a slave, and these revelations being made known to me, I began to direct my attention to this great object, to fulfil the purpose for which, by this time, I felt assured I was intended. Knowing the influence I had obtained over the minds

135

of my fellow servants, (not by the means of conjuring and such like tricks—for to them I always spoke of such things with contempt) but by the communion of the Spirit whose revelations I often communicated to them, and they believed and said my wisdom came from God. I now began to prepare them for my purpose, by telling them something was about to happen that would terminate in fulfilling the great promise that had been made to me—About this time I was placed under an overseer, from whom I ranaway—and after remaining in the woods thirty days, I returned, to the astonishment of the negroes on the plantation, who thought I had made my escape to some other part of the country, as my father had done before. But the reason of my return was, that the Spirit appeared to me and said I had my wishes directed to the things of this world, and not to the kingdom of Heaven, and that I should return to the service of my earthly master—"For he who knoweth his Master's will, and doeth it not, shall be beaten with many stripes, and thus have I chastened you." And the negroes found fault, and murmured against me, saying that if they had my sense they would not serve any master in the world. And about this time I had a vision—and I saw white spirits and black spirits engaged in battle, and the sun was darkened—the thunder rolled in the Heavens, and blood flowed in streams —and I heard a voice saying, "Such is your luck, such you are called to see, and let it come rough or smooth, you must surely bare it. I now withdrew myself as much as my situation would permit, from the intercourse of my fellow servants, for the avowed purpose of serving the Spirit more fully— and it appeared to me, and reminded me of the things it had already shown me, and that it would then reveal to me the knowledge of the elements, the revolution of the planets, the operation of tides, and changes of the seasons. After this revelation in the year of 1825, and the knowledge of the elements being made known to me, I sought more than ever to obtain true holiness before the great day of judgment should appear, and then I began to receive the true knowledge of faith. And from the first steps of righteouness until the last, was I made perfect; and the Holy Ghost was with me, and said, "Behold me as I stand in the Heavens"— and I looked and saw the forms of men in different attitudes— and there were lights in the sky to which the children of darkness gave other names than what they really were—for they were the lights of the Savior's hands, stretched forth from east to west, even as they were extended on the cross on Calvary for the redemption of sinners. And I wondered greatly at these miracles, and prayed to be informed of a certainty of the meaning thereof—and shortly afterwards, while laboring in the field, I discovered drops of blood on the corn as though it were dew from heaven—and I communicated it to many, both white and black, in the neighborhood—and I then found on the leaves in the woods hieroglyphic characters, and numbers, with the forms of men in different attitudes, portrayed in blood, and representing the figures I had seen before in the heavens. And now the Holy Ghost had revealed itself to me, and made plain the miracles it had shown me—For as the blood of Christ had been shed on this earth, and had ascended to heaven for the salvation of sinners, and was now returning to earth again in the form of dew—and as the leaves on the trees bore the impression of the figures I had seen in the heavens, it was plain to me that the Savior was about to lay down the yoke he had borne for the sins of men, and the great day of judgment was at hand. About this time I told these things to a white man, (Etheldred T. Brantley) on whom it had a wonderful effect—and he ceased from his wickedness, and was attacked immediately with a cutaneous eruption, and blood oozed from the pores of his skin, and after praying and fasting nine days, he was healed, and the Spirit appeared to me again, and said, as the Savior had been baptised so should we be also—and when the white people would not let us be baptised by the church, we went down into the water together, in the sight of many who reviled us, and were baptised by the Spirit—After this I rejoiced greatly, and gave thanks to God. And on the 12th of May, 1828, I heard a loud noise in the heavens, and the Spirit instantly appeared to me and said the Serpent was loosened, and Christ had laid down the yoke he had borne for the sins of men, and that I should take it on and fight against the Serpent, for the time was fast approaching when the first should be last and the last should be first. *Ques.* Do you not find yourself mistaken now? *Ans.* Was not Christ crucified? And by signs in the heavens that it would make known to me when I should commence the great work—and until the first sign appeared, I should conceal it from the knowledge of men—And on the appearance of the sign, (the eclipse of the sun last February) I should arise and prepare myself, and slay my enemies with their own weapons. And immediately on the sign appearing in the heavens, the seal was removed from my lips, and I communicated the great work laid out for me to do, to four in whom I had the greatest confidence, (Henry, Hark, Nelson, and Sam)—It was intended by us to have begun the work of death on the 4th July last—Many were the plans formed and rejected by us, and it affected my mind to such a degree, that I fell sick, and the time passed without our coming to any determination how to commence—Still forming new schemes and rejecting them, when the sign appeared again, which determined me not to wait longer.

Since the commencement of 1830, I had been living with Mr. Joseph Travis, who was to me a kind master, and placed the greatest confidence in me; in fact, I had no cause to complain of his treatment to me. On Saturday evening, the 20th of August, it was agreed between Henry, Hark and myself, to prepare a dinner the next day for the men we expected, and then to concert a plan, as we had not yet determined on any. Hark, on the following morning, brought a pig, and Henry brandy, and being joined by Sam, Nelson, Will and

Jack, they prepared in the woods a dinner, where, about three o'clock, I joined them.

Q. Why were you so backward in joining them.

A. The same reason that had caused me not to mix with them for years before.

I saluted them on coming up, and asked Will how came he there, he answered, his life was worth no more than others, and his liberty as dear to him. I asked him if he thought to obtain it? He said he would, or lose his life. This was enough to put him in full confidence. Jack, I knew, was only a tool in the hands of Hark, it was quickly agreed we should commence at home (Mr. J. Travis') on that night, and until we had armed and equipped ourselves, and gathered sufficient force, neither age nor sex was to be spared, (which was invariably adhered to). We remained at the feast, until about two hours in the night, when we went to the house and found Austin; they all went to the cider press and drank, except myself. On returning to the house, Hark went to the door with an axe, for the purpose of breaking it open, as we knew we were strong enough to murder the family, if they were awaked by the noise; but reflecting that it might create an alarm in the neighborhood, we determined to enter the house secretly, and murder them whilst sleeping. Hark got a ladder and set it against the chimney, on which I ascended, and hoisting a window, entered and came down stairs, unbarred the door, and removed the guns from their places. It was then observed that I must spill the first blood. On which, armed with a hatchet, and accompanied by Will, I entered my master's chamber, it being dark, I could not give a death blow, the hatchet glanced from his head, he sprang from the bed and called his wife, it was his last word, Will laid him dead, with a blow of his axe, and Mrs. Travis shared the same fate, as she lay in bed. The murder of this family, five in number, was the work of a moment, not one of them awoke; there was a little infant sleeping in a cradle, that was forgotten, until

139

we had left the house and gone some distance, when Henry and Will returned and killed it; we got here, four guns that would shoot, and several old muskets, with a pound or two of powder. We remained some time at the barn, where we paraded; I formed them in a line as soldiers, and after carrying them through all the manoeuvres I was master of marched them off to Mr. Salathul Francis', about six hundred yards distant. Sam and Will went to the door and knocked. Mr. Francis asked who was there, Sam replied it was him, and he had a letter for him, on which he got up and came to the door; they immediately seized him, and dragging him out a little from the door, he was dispatched by repeated blows on the head; there was no other white person in the family. We started from there for Mrs. Reese's, maintaining the most perfect silence on our march, where finding the door unlocked, we entered, and murdered Mrs. Reese in her bed, while sleeping; her son awoke, but it was only to sleep the sleep of death, he had only time to say who is that, and he was no more. From Mrs. Reese's we went to Mrs. Turner's, a mile distant, which we reached about sunrise, on Monday morning. Henry, Austin, and Sam, went to the still, where, finding Mr. Peebles, Austin shot him, and the rest of us went to the house; as we approached, the family discovered us, and shut the door. Vain hope! Will, with one stroke of his axe, opened it, and we entered and found Mrs. Turner and Mrs. Newsome in the middle of a room, almost frightened to death. Will immediately killed Mrs. Turner, with one blow of his axe. I took Mrs. Newsome by the hand, and with the sword I had when I was apprehended, I struck her several blows over the head, but not being able to kill her, as the sword was dull. Will turning around and discovering it, despatched her also. A general destruction of property and search for money and ammunition, always succeded the murders. By this time my company amounted to fifteen, and nine men mounted, who started for Mrs. Whitehead's, (the other six were to go through a by way to Mr. Bryant's, and rejoin us at Mrs. Whitehead's,) as we approached the house we discovered Mr. Richard Whitehead standing in the cotton patch, near the lane fence; we called him over into the lane, and Will, the executioner, was near at hand, with his fatal axe, to send him to an untimely grave. As we pushed on to the house, I discovered some one run round the garden, and thinking it was some of the white family, I pursued them, but finding it was a servant girl belonging to the house, I returned to commence the work of death, but they whom I left, had not been idle; all the family were already murdered, but Mrs. Whitehead and her daughter Margaret. As I came round to the door I saw Will pulling Mrs. Whitehead out of the house, and at the step he nearly severed her head from her body, with his broad axe. Miss Margaret, when I discovered her, had concealed herself in the corner, formed by the projection of cellar cap from the house; on my approach she fled, but was soon overtaken, and after repeated blows with a sword, I killed her by a blow on the head, with a fence rail. By this time, the six who had gone by Mr. Bryant's, rejoined us, and informed me they had done the work of death assigned them. We again divided, part going to Mr. Richard Porter's, and from thence to Nathaniel Francis', the others to Mr. Howell Harris', and Mr. T. Doyles. On my reaching Mr. Porter's, he had escaped with his family. I understood there, that the alarm had already spread, and I immediately returned to bring up those sent to Mr. Doyles, and Mr. Howell Harris'; the party I left going on to Mr. Francis', having told them I would join them in that neighborhood. I met these sent to Mr. Doyles' and Mr. Harris' returning, having met Mr. Doyle on the road and killed him; and learning from some who joined them, that Mr. Harris was from home, I immediately pursued the course taken by the party gone on before; but knowing they would complete the work of death and pillage, at Mr. Francis' before I could get there, I went to Mr. Peter

141

Edwards', expecting to find them there, but they had been here also. I then went to Mr. John T. Barrow's, they had been here and murdered him. I pursued on their track to Capt. Newit Harris', where I found the greater part mounted, and ready to start; the men now amounting to about forty, shouted and hurraed as I rode up, some were in the yard, loading their guns, others drinking. They said Captain Harris and his family had escaped, the property in the house they destroyed, robbing him of money and other valuables. I ordered them to mount and march instantly, this was about nine or ten o'clock, Monday morning. I proceeded to Mr. Levi Waller's, two or three miles distant. I took my station in the rear, and as it was my object to carry terror and devastation wherever we went, I placed fifteen or twenty of the best armed and most relied on, in front, who generally approached the houses as fast as their horses could run; this was for two purposes, to prevent escape and strike terror to the inhabitants—on this account I never got to the houses, after leaving Mrs. Whitehead's, until the murders were committed, except in one case. I sometimes got in sight in time to see the work of death completed, viewed the mangled bodies as they lay, in silent satisfaction, and immediately started in quest of other victims—Having murdered Mrs. Waller and ten children, we started for Mr. William Williams'—having killed him and two little boys that were there; while engaged in this, Mrs. Williams fled and got some distance from the house, but she was pursued, overtaken, and compelled to get up behind one of the company, who brought her back, and after showing her the mangled body of her lifeless husband, she was told to get down and lay by his side, where she was shot dead. I then started for Mr. Jacob Williams, where the family were murdered—Here he found a young man named Drury, who had come on business with Mr. Williams—he was pursued, overtaken and shot. Mrs. Vaughan was the next place we visited—and after murdering the family here, I determined on starting for

Jerusalem—Our number amounted now to fifty or sixty, all mounted and armed with guns, axes, swords and clubs—On reaching Mr. James W. Parker's gate, immediately on the road leading to Jerusalem, and about three miles distant, it was proposed to me to call there, but I objected, as I knew he was gone to Jerusalem, and my object was to reach there as soon as possible; but some of the men having relations at Mr. Parker's it was agreed that they might call and get his people. I remained at the gate on the road, with seven or eight; the others going across the field to the house, about half a mile off. After waiting some time for them, I became impatient, and started to the house for them, and on our return we were met by a party of white when, who had pursued our blood-stained track, and who had fired on those at the gate, and dispersed them, which I knew nothing of, not having been at that time rejoined by any of them—Immediately on discovering the whites, I ordered my men to halt and form, as they appeared to be alarmed—The white men, eighteen in number, approached us in about one hundred yards, when one of them fired, (this was against the positive orders of Captain Alexander P. Peete, who commanded, and who had directed the men to reserve their fire until within thirty paces) —And I discovered about half of them retreating, I then ordered my men to fire and rush on them; the few remaining stood their ground until we approached within fifty yards, when they fired and retreated. We pursued and overtook some of them who we thought we left dead; (they were not killed) after pursuing them about two hundred yards, and rising a little hill, I discovered they were met by another party, and had halted, and were re-loading their guns, (this was a small party from Jerusalem who knew the negroes were in the field, and had just tied their horses to await their return to the road, knowing that Mr. Parker and family were in Jerusalem, but knew nothing of the party that had gone in with Captain Peete; on hearing the firing they immediately rushed to the spot and arrived just in time to arrest the progress of these barbarous villians, and save the lives of their friends and fellow citizens). Thinking that those who retreated first, and the party who fired on us at fifty or sixty yards distant, had all fallen back to meet others with ammunition. As I saw them reloading their guns, and more coming up than I saw at first, and several of my bravest men being wounded, the others became panick struck and squandered over the field; the white men pursued and fired on us several times. Hark had his horse shot under him, and I caught another for him as it was running by me; five or six of my men were wounded, but none left on the field; finding myself defeated here I instantly determined to go through a private way, and cross the Nottoway river at the Cypress Bridge, three miles below Jerusalem, and attack that place in the rear, as I expected they would look for me on the other road, and I had a great desire to get there to procure arms and ammunition. After going a short distance in this private way, accompanied by about twenty men, I overtook two or three who told me the others were dispersed in every direction. After trying in vain to collect a sufficient force to proceed to Jerusalem, I determined to return, as I was sure they would make back to their old neighborhood, where they would rejoin me, make new recruits, and come down again. On my way back, I called at Mrs. Thomas's, Mrs. Spencer's, and several other places, the white families having fled, we found no more victims to gratify our thirst for blood, we stopped at Majr. Ridley's quarter for the night, and being joined by four of his men, with the recruits made since my defeat, we mustered now about forty strong. After placing out sentinels, I laid down to sleep, but was quickly roused by a great racket; starting up, I found some mounted, and others in great confusion; one of the sentinels having given the alarm that we were about to be attacked, I ordered some to ride round and reconnoitre, and on their return the others being more alarmed, not knowing who they were, fled in different ways, so that I was reduced to about twenty again; with this I determined to attempt to recruit, and proceed on to rally in the neighborhood, I had left. Dr. Blunt's was the nearest house, which we reached just before day; on riding up the yard, Hark fired a gun. We expected Dr. Blunt and his family were at Maj. Ridley's, as I knew there was a company of men there; the gun was fired to ascertain if any of the family were at home; we were immediately fired upon and retreated, leaving several of my men. I do not know what became of them, as I never saw them afterwards. Pursuing our course back and coming in sight of Captain Harris', where we had been the day before, we discovered a party of white men at the house, on which all deserted me but two, (Jacob and Nat), we concealed ourselves in the woods until near night, when I sent them in search of Henry, Sam, Nelson, and Hark, and directed them to rally all they could, at the place we had had our dinner the Sunday before, where they would find me, and I accordingly returned there as soon as it was dark and remained until Wednesday evening, when discovering white men riding around the place as though they were looking for some one, and none of my men joining me, I concluded Jacob and Nat had been taken, and compelled to betray me. On this I gave up all hope for the present; and on Thursday night after having supplied myself with provisions from Mr. Travis's, I scratched a hole under a pile of fence rails in a field, where I concealed myself for six weeks, never leaving my hiding place but for a few minutes in the dead of night to get water which was very near; thinking by this time I could venture out, I began to go about in the night and eaves drop the houses in the neighborhood; pursuing this course for about a fortnight and gathering little or no intelligence, afraid of speaking to any human being, and returning every morning to my cave before the dawn of day. I know not how long I might have led this life, if accident had not betrayed me, a dog in the neighborhood passing by my hiding place one night while I was out, was attracted by some meat I had in my cave, and crawled in and stole it, and was coming out just as I returned. A few nights after, two negroes having started to go hunting with the same dog, and passed that way, the dog came again to the place, and having just gone out to walk about, discovered me and barked, on which thinking myself discovered, I spoke to them to beg concealment. On making myself known they fled from me. Knowing then they would betray me, I immediately left my hiding place, and was pursued almost incessantly until I was taken a fortnight afterwards by Mr. Benjamin Phipps, in a little hole I had dug out with my sword, for the purpose of concealment, under the top of a fallen tree. On Mr. Phipps' discovering the place of my concealment, he cocked his gun and aimed at me. I requested him not to shoot and I would give up, upon which he demanded my sword. I delivered it to him, and he brought me to prison. During the time I was pursued, I had many hair breadth escapes, which your time will not permit you to relate. I am here loaded with chains, and willing to suffer the fate that awaits me.

I here proceeded to make some inquiries of him, after assuring him of the certain death that awaited him, and that concealment would only bring destruction on the innocent as well as guilty, of his own color, if he knew of any extensive or concerted plan. His answer was, I do not. When I questioned him as to the insurrection in North Carolina happening about the same time, he denied any knowledge of it; and when I looked him in the face as though I would search his inmost thoughts, he replied, "I see sir, you doubt my word; but can you not think the same ideas, and strange appearances about this time in the heaven's might prompt others, as well as myself, to this undertaking." I now had much conversation with and asked him many questions, having forborne to do so previously, except in the cases noted in parenthesis; but during his statement, I had, unnoticed by him, taken notes as to some particular circumstances, and having the advantage of his statement before me in writing, on the evening of the third day that I had been with him, I began a cross examination, and found his statement corroborated by every circumstance coming within my own knowledge or the confessions of others who had been either killed or executed, and whom he had not seen nor had any knowledge since 22d of August last, he expressed himself fully satisfied as to the impracticability of his attempt. It has been said he was ignorant and cowardly, and that his object was to murder and rob for the purpose of obtaining money to make his escape. It is notorious, that he was never known to have a dollar in his life; to swear an oath, or drink a drop of spirits. As to his ignorance, he certainly never had the advantages of education, but he can read and write, (it was taught him by his parents,) and for natural intelligence and quickness of apprehension, is surpassed by few men I have ever seen. As to his being a coward, his reason as given for not resisting Mr. Phipps, shews the decision of his character. When he saw Mr. Phipps present his gun, he said he knew it was impossible for him to escape as the woods were full of men; he therefore thought it was better to surrender, and trust to fortune for his escape. He is a complete fanatic, or plays his part most admirably. On other subjects he possesses an uncommon share of intelligence, with a mind capable of attaining any thing; but warped and perverted by the influence of early impressions. He is below the ordinary stature, though strong and active, having the true negro face, every feature of which is strongly marked. I shall not attempt to describe the effect of his narrative, as told and commented on by himself, in the condemned hole of the prison. The calm, deliberate composure with which he spoke of his late deeds and intentions, the expression of his fiend like face when excited by enthusiasm, still bearing the stains of the blood of helpless innocence about him; clothed with rags and

147

covered with chains; yet daring to raise his manacled hands to heaven, with a spirit soaring above the attributes of man; I looked on him and my blood curdled in my veins.

I will not shock the feelings of humanity, nor wound afresh the bosoms of the disconsolate sufferers in this unparalleled and inhuman massacre, by detailing the deeds of their fiend-like barbarity. There were two or three who were in the power of these wretches, had they known it, and who escaped in the most providential manner. There were two whom they thought they left dead on the field at Mr. Parker's, but who were only stunned by the blows of their guns, as they did not take time to re-load when they charged on them. The escape of a little girl who went to school at Mr. Waller's, and where the children were collecting for that purpose, excited general sympathy. As their teacher had not arrived, they were at play in the yard, and seeing the negroes approach, she ran up on a dirt chimney, (such as are common to log houses,) and remained there unnoticed during the massacre of the eleven that were killed at this place. She remained on her hiding place till just before the arrival of a party, who were in pursuit of the murderers, when she came down and fled to a swamp, where, a mere child as she was, with the horrors of the late scene before her, she lay concealed until the next day, when seeing a party go up to the house, she came up, and on being asked how she escaped, replied with the utmost simplicity, "The Lord helped her." She was taken up behind a gentleman of the party, and returned to the arms of her weeping mother. Miss Whitehead concealed herself between the bed and the mat that supported it, while they murdered her sister in the same room, without discovering her. She was afterwards carried off, and concealed for protection by a slave of the family, who gave evidence against several of them on their trial. Mrs. Nathaniel Francis, while concealed in a closet heard their blows, and the shrieks of the victims of these ruthless savages; they then entered the closet, where she was concealed, and went out without discovering her. While in this hiding place, she heard two of her women in a quarrel about the division of her clothes. Mr. John T. Baron, discovering them approaching his house, told his wife to make her escape, and scorning to fly, fell fighting on his own threshold. After firing his rifle, he discharged his gun at them, and then broke it over the villain who first approached him, but he was overpowered, and slain. His bravery, however, saved from the hands of these monsters, his lovely and amiable wife, who will long lament a husband so deserving of her love. As directed by him, she attempted to escape through the garden, when she was caught and held by one of her servant girls, but another coming to her rescue, she fled to the woods, and concealed herself. Few indeed, were those who escaped their work of death. But fortunate for society, the hand of retributive justice has overtaken them; and not one that was known to be concerned has escaped.

The Commonwealth,
      vs.
    Nat Turner

                Charged with making insurrection, and plotting to take away the lives of divers free white persons,

&c. on the 22d of August, 1831.

The court composed of ——, having met for the trial of Nat Turner, the prisoner was brought in and arraigned, and upon his arraignment pleaded *Not guilty;* saying to his counsel, that he did not feel so.

On the part of the Commonwealth, Levi Waller was introduced, who being sworn, deposed as follows: (*agreeably to Nat's own Confession.*) Col. Trezvant* was then in-

---

*The committing Magistrate.

troduced, who being sworn, narrated Nat's Confession to him, as follows: (*his Confession as given to Mr. Gray.*) The prisoner introduced no evidence, and the case was submitted without argument to the court, who having found him guilty, Jeremiah Cobb, Esq. Chairman, pronounced the sentence of the court, in the following words: Nat Turner! Stand up. Have you any thing to say why sentence of death should not be pronounced against you?

Ans. I have not. I have made a full confession to Mr. Gray, and I have nothing more to say.

Attend then to the sentence of the Court. You have been arraigned and tried before this court, and convicted of one of the highest crimes in our criminal code. You have been convicted of plotting in cold blood, the indiscriminate destruction of men, of helpless women, and of infant children. The evidence before us leaves not a shadow of doubt, but that your hands were often imbrued in the blood of the innocent; and your own confession tells us that they were stained with the blood of a master; in your own language, "too indulgent." Could I stop here, your crime would be sufficiently aggravated. But the original contriver of a plan, deep and deadly, one that never can be effected, you managed so far to put it into execution, as to deprive us of many of our most valuable citizens; and this was done when they were asleep, and defenseless; under circumstances shocking to humanity. And while upon this part of the subject, I cannot but call your attention to the poor misguided wretches who have gone before you. They are not few in number—they were your bosom associates; and the blood of all cries aloud, and calls upon you, as the author of their misfortune. Yes! You forced them unprepared, from Time to Eternity. Borne down by this load of guilt, your only justification is, that you were led away by fanaticism. If this be true, from my soul I pity you; and while you have my sympathies, I am, nevertheless called upon to pass the sentence of the court. The time between this and your execution, will necessarily be very short; and your only hope must be in another world. The judgment of the court is, that you be taken hence to the jail from whence you came, thence to the place of execution, and on Friday next, between the hours of 10 A.M. and 2 P.M. be hung by the neck until you are dead! dead! dead! and may the Lord have mercy upon your soul.

A list of persons murdered in the Insurrection, on the 21st and 22nd of August, 1831.

Joseph Travers and wife and three children, Mrs. Elizabeth Turner, Hartwell Prebles, Sarah Newsome, Mrs. P. Reese and son William, Trajan Doyle, Henry Bryant and wife and child, and wife's mother, Mrs. Catharine Whitehead, son Richard and four daughters and grand-child, Salathiel Francis, Nathaniel Francis' overseer and two children, John T. Barrow, George Vaughan, Mrs. Levi Waller and ten children, William Williams, wife and two boys, Mrs. Caswell Worrell and child, Mrs. Rebecca Vaughan, Ann Eliza Vaughan, and son Arthur, Mrs. John K. Williams and child, Mrs. Jacob Williams and three children, and Edwin Drury—amounting to fifty-five.

A *List of Negroes brought before the Court of Southampton,* *with their owners' names, and sentence.*

Daniel,	Richard Porter,	Convicted.
Moses	J. T. Barrow,	do.
Tom,	Caty Whitehead,	Discharged.
Jack and Andrew,	Caty Whitehead	Con. and transported
Jacob,	Geo. H. Charlton,	Disch'd without trial.
Isaac,	Ditto,	Convi. and transported.
Jack,	Everett Bryant,	Discharged.
Nathan,	Benj. Blunt's estate,	Convicted.
Nathan, Tom, and	Nathaniel Francis,	Convicted and transported
Davy, (boys,)	Elizabeth Turner,	Convicted.
Davy,	Thomas Ridley,	Do.
Curtis,	Do.	Do.
Stephen,	Benjamin Edwards,	Convicted and transp'd.
Hardy and Isham,	Nathaniel Francis,	Convicted.
Sam,	Joseph Travis' estate.	Do.
Hark,	Do.	Do. and transported.
Moses, (a boy,)	Levi Waller,	Convicted.
Davy,	Jacob Williams,	Do.
Nelson,	Edm'd Turner's estate	Do.
Nat,	Wm. Reese's estate	Do.
Dred,	Nathaniel Francis,	Do.
Arnold, Artist, (free)		Discharged.
Sam,	J. W. Parker,	Acquitted.
Ferry and Archer,	J. W. Parker,	Disch'd. without trial.
Jim,	William Vaughan,	Acquitted.
Bob,	Temperance Parker,	Do.
Davy,	Joseph Parker,	
Daniel,	Solomon D. Parker	Disch'd without trial.
Thomas Haithcock, (free,)		Sent on for further trial.
Joe,	John C. Turner,	Convicted.
Lucy,	John T. Barrow,	Do.
Matt,	Thomas Ridley,	Acquitted.
Jim,	Richard Porter,	Do.
Exum Artes, (free,)		Sent on for further trial.
Joe,	Richard P. Briggs,	Disch'd without trial.
Bury Newsome, (free,)		Sent on for further trial.
Stephen,	James Bell,	Acquitted.
Jim and Isaac,	Samuel Champion,	Convicted and trans'd.
Preston,	Hannah Williamson	Acquitted.
Frank,	Solomon D. Parker	Convi'd and transp'd.
Jack and Shadrach,	Nathaniel Simmons	Acquitted.
Nelson,	Benj. Blunt's estate,	Do.
Sam,	Peter Edwards,	Convicted.
Archer,	Arthur G. Reese,	Acquitted.
Isham Turner, (free,)		Sent on for further trial.
Nat Turner,	Putnam Moore, dec'd.	Convicted.

Nat Turner Slave Revolt
Nat Turner ~~state~~ confessions
while...locked in prison
Nat Turner "Confessions"

CO